"This small book contains big ideas about active learning, both online and in-person. Kosslyn bridges his knowledge of cognitive science with his experience in two education technology start-ups to provide a pedagogical handbook of sorts. Using engaging research studies, Kosslyn begins with an overview of basic cognitive functions, specifically how we organize, store and access information in memory. From here, he presents his own taxonomy of five learning principles: deep processing, chunking, associations, dual coding and deliberate practice. Then comes the lesson for instructors, as we come to appreciate exercises grounded in these principles. After reading this book, you will abandon the lecture for a brief lecture followed by active learning exercises, for example asking students to teach another student, to take the perspective or others through role playing or debate, to create content like a podcast and more. If your goal is to teach to make material stick with your students, and it should be, this book will be your guide."

Kathleen McCartney, *President, Smith College*

"Stephen Kosslyn, one of the world's leading researchers on the science of learning, provides practical, easy-to-use methods that help students learn more effectively -- especially online, synchronously and asynchronously, and at scale. This book is an invaluable tool for all educators, and an enlightening resource for anyone interested in improving current education practices."

Jeff Maggioncalda, *CEO, Coursera*

"Every parent and student who were already online learners or who have been pushed by the pandemic into the online world should read this book. Professor Kosslyn has dedicated his academic life to the study of how human beings learn and has developed extremely valuable lessons in how to thrive in a virtual classroom."

Bob Kerrey, *former U.S. Senator; President Emeritus, The New School*

"Active learning is a good idea that's rarely implemented. Stephen Kosslyn makes here a persuasive case for its adoption and gives a straightforward plan to create more engaging and effective courses. That's no surprise, because he effortlessly combines enormous insight and experience into creative solutions."

John Katzman, *Founder and CEO of Noodle, and Founder and Former CEO of 2U and Princeton Review*

"I cannot tell you how excited I am by this book! It absolutely is my go-to recommendation in the space and is required reading for our whole curriculum team. It's the perfect combination of theory and application with 0% fluff. I was familiar with many of the concepts in it, but only after ridiculous amounts of reading and discussions around the topic. This seems to be the exact slice of the field someone needs to actually build a class with the best teaching techniques in active learning."

Aaron Rasmussen, *Founder and CEO of Outlier.org, Co-Founder of MasterClass*

D0108185

"How do we ensure online learning lives up to its promise and potential? In Active Learning Online, Stephen Kosslyn equips educators everywhere by delivering fresh perspectives on the science of learning along with practical ways they can be applied in real life courses. For all the years I've been involved in adult learning and active learning, this book still surprised me with brilliant insights and made me think about how to implement his ideas."

Mary Hawkins, *President, Bellevue University*

"This is a phenomenally readable, concise and efficient summary of the current science of active learning and how it can improve your teaching. It is full of useful examples and clear explanations. While most of illuminating suggestions are applied to online teaching, the practical advice here will also easily be applied to any teaching situation. There is no better overview of this exploding field and there could not be a better time for this book. Read it in a morning and have your teaching transformed by the afternoon."

José Bowen, *President Emeritus, Goucher College*

"At last—a book that summarizes principles from the learning sciences that is at once both accessible and actionable! Any educator at any skill level will be able to derive value from Kosslyn's valuable contribution to improve the experience they offer students."

Michael B. Horn, *coauthor of* Choosing College *and Co-Founder of the Clayton Christensen Institute*

"Active Learning Online is an extraordinary work that will revolutionize the way you think about education, and will shape both educational practice and conversations about effective education for many years and decades to come."

Daniel J. Levitin, *author of bestsellers* This Is Your Brain on Music, The Organized Mind, *and* Successful Aging

---

"Drawing skillfully on a lifetime of teaching, conducting research, and leading educational institutions, cognitive psychologist Stephen Kosslyn distills the key components of effective education—on line, as well as in the "live" classroom. This book is timely and should be useful for any instructor."

Howard Gardner, *Hobbs Research Professor of Cognition and Education, Harvard Graduate School of Education*

Active Learning Online

Five Principles that Make Online Courses Come Alive

Stephen M. Kosslyn

ALINEA

Alinea Learning
Boston

ALINEA

Alinea Learning

Boston, Massachusetts

Published in the United States by Alinea Learning,
an imprint and division of Alinea Knowledge, LLC, Boston.

Visit our website at **www.alinealearning.org**.

Library of Congress Cataloging-in-Publication Data is available on file.

Print book ISBN: 978-1-7358107-0-6

eBook ISBN: 978-1-7358107-1-3

Cover design by Imprudent Press LLC

Cover copyright © 2021 by Alinea Knowledge, LLC

Contents

Preface   v

About the Author   ix

1 What Is Active Learning and Why Is It Important?   1

Should Lectures Be Banned?   6

The "Learning Sandwich": Synchronous and Asynchronous Settings   9

2 The Science of Learning   19

Key Facts about the Brain: Foundations of the Principles   21

3 Deep Processing   27

Targeted Processing   30

Finding the Goldilocks Spot   34

4 Chunking   39

Using Chunking to Organize Lessons   42

5 Building Associations   45

Designing Lessons   47

Spaced Practice and Varied Context   48

Organizing Examples   50

6   Dual Coding   53

Illustrating Concepts   54
Using Charts, Graphs and Diagrams   56
Visualizing Illustrations   59

7   Deliberate Practice   61

Selectively Paying Attention   64
Deliberate Practice at Scale   65

8   Combining Principles   71

Elaboration, Generation Effect, Testing Effect   75
Games and Meta-Cognition   76

9   Intrinsic and Extrinsic Motivation   79

Intrinsic Motivation   80
Extrinsic Motivation   83
Different Types of Incentives and Consequences   84
Social Motivation Online   89

10   Exercises and Activities   91

Specific Exercises   91
Formats for Online Active Learning   97

Preface

This book grew out of decades of research, reflection, and personal experience building new teaching methods based on the science of learning. I had the good fortune to oversee the design of the academic programs of not one, but two new institutions of higher education, the Minerva Schools at KGI (as Founding Dean and Chief Academic Officer) and then Foundry College (as President and Chief Academic Officer). These both were extraordinary and rare opportunities to take a step back and ask big questions about what education is for and how best to accomplish those aims.

How did I find myself designing curricula for new institutions? I earned a Ph.D. at Stanford University during the birth of cognitive science and was the first cognitive psychologist hired in the faculty of Arts and Sciences at Harvard University. My research focused on visual mental imagery, which led me to study perception and memory. I wrote books on these topics, as well as books on how to apply psychology to visual display design and to making better PowerPoint presentations. I published over 300 research articles on these and related topics and co-authored four textbooks that span a wide range of material in psychology and cognitive science. The nature and mechanisms of learning were at the heart of all of this, and I continually found myself thinking about how to use what we know to good ends. After decades of being a traditional academic, I decided that I wanted to see this knowledge used to help students learn. This led me to leave traditional academia and dive into the startup world. If nothing else, working for a startup has been a learning experience!

The material in this book is firmly at the intersection of the science of learning and EdTech startups. I was able to develop and refine this material by devising ways to help our students learn and observing the outcomes. This experience has resulted in many teaching techniques, which students have received well. Most recently, the students at Foundry College have given the program a Net Promoter Score over 60 for the past four trimesters (which is extremely high).

In the course of actually using the principles in the classroom at Foundry College, I've been led to change my views on several topics.

First, during my time at Minerva I was adamantly opposed to lectures.[1] With additional reading, reflection, and experience I have since come to realize that lectures have a place, as I describe in this book.

Second, I had previously organized the empirical literature on the science of learning into 16 principles,[2] which in practice proved unwieldy and somewhat confusing; when using the principles extensively, I realized that some of them overlapped and some actually addressed specific aspects of others. Mulling this over for several years, I finally was able to reorganize this material into just five principles, as summarized in this book.

Third, I previously had focused solely on "practical knowledge," which I still think is important. However, I appreciate the value of having a lot of tools in the toolkit, standing in reserve for unpredictable contingencies and opportunities that the future may bring. Thus, in this book I focus more generally on ways to help students learn knowledge and skills—including those that are the lifeblood of traditional liberal arts programs.

This book could not have been written without the help of many people who reviewed an earlier draft and helped me be clearer and more accurate. First, I thank Dr. Beth Callaghan (a fantastic collaborator at both Minerva and then at Foundry College, a master teacher and excellent writer), Laurence Holt (one of the smartest, broadest educators I have ever met), Dr. Richard Robb (economist and thinker extraordinaire with a keen eye and excellent taste), Justin Kosslyn (one of the clearest thinkers I've ever known who leavens his critiques with wry humor), Dr. Kacey Warren (who uses her analytic philosophy background to good end and is a master of online instruction), Dr. Melora Sundt (who has been on the front lines of online education for years, and is deeply immersed in literatures I had barely heard of), Dr. Kathy Hanson (who has an extraordinarily broad perspective and helped me understand the intricacies of Zoom), and Maria Anguiano (Board member at Foundry College, mover-and-shaker in higher ed and all-around smart and wise person). I am flattered and extremely grateful that these very busy and accomplished people took the time to give me comments and suggestions (and even went so far as to suggest specific revisions in some places). This book is

---

1   See Kosslyn, S. M., & Nelson, B. (2017). *Building the intentional university: Minerva and the future of higher education.* Cambridge, MA: MIT Press.

2   Kosslyn, S. M. (2017). The science of learning. In S. M. Kosslyn & B. Nelson (Eds.), *Building the intentional university: Minerva and the future of higher education.* Cambridge, MA: MIT Press.

far better for their efforts, but they of course bear no responsibility for flaws that still remain.

Next I thank my wife, Dr. Robin S. Rosenberg, who took time from running her virtual reality inclusion-and-diversity startup, coaching practice and clinical psychology practice to provide sage and smart advice and guidance. And I also thank her brother, Steven Rosenberg, who understands systems better than I ever will and has been incredibly generous with his time and astute counsel. My other two sons, Neil and David, also provided advice that helped guide this project. I also must express my gratitude to the team at Alinea Learning, who believed in this book and accepted it to be the first publication of their new press. Finally, I thank my colleagues at Foundry College, who gave me the space to write this book and have been so open to incorporating many of these ideas into the curriculum.

About the Author

Stephen M. Kosslyn is currently the Founder, President and Chief Academic Officer of Foundry College and is Founder and President of Active Learning Sciences. Prior to that, he was Founding Dean and Chief Academic Officer of the Minerva Schools at the Keck Graduate Institute. He previously served as Director of the Center for Advanced Study in the Behavioral Sciences at Stanford University after having been chair of the Department of Psychology, Dean of Social Science, and the John Lindsley Professor of Psychology at Harvard University. While at Harvard, he was also co-director of the Mind of the Market Lab at Harvard Business School and a member of the Department of Neurology at the Massachusetts General Hospital. He received a B.A. from UCLA and a Ph.D. from Stanford University, both in psychology. Kosslyn's research has focused on the nature of visual cognition, visual communication, and the science of learning; he has authored or coauthored 14 books and over 300 papers on these topics. Kosslyn has received numerous honors, including the National Academy of Sciences Initiatives in Research Award, a Guggenheim Fellowship, three honorary Doctorates (University of Caen, University of Paris Descartes, Bern University), and election to the American Academy of Arts and Sciences.

—1—

What Is Active Learning and Why Is It Important?

The Spring of 2020 witnessed a massive unplanned experiment in online education. Covid-19 forced schools, at all levels covering all topics, to go online with very little warning or preparation. Across the globe, video conferencing platforms (most notably, Google Meet, Webex and—especially—Zoom) were pressed into service to teach courses. The results were not optimal. As a *Wall Street Journal* headline concluded: "The results are in for remote learning: It didn't work."[3]

It didn't work for the same reason we don't watch movies from the 1910s. The producers simply pointed a camera at traditional plays, failing to tap the world of possibilities opened up by the new technology. The first movies were "stagey."

A traditional lecture on a video conferencing platform offers all the defects of a lecture minus the immediacy of personal contact. But just as the movies went on to bring wonders not imagined 100 years ago, online courses can be vastly better. Fortunately, the know-how, informed by the science of learning, is here and ready to be used.

---

3 Hobbs, T. D., & Hawkins, L. (2020, June 5). The results are in for remote learning: It didn't work. *Wall Street Journal*: https://www.wsj.com/articles/schools-coronavirus-remote-learning-lockdown-tech-11591375078

Although the rush to teach online in the Spring of 2020 was unprecedented, it simply accelerated a trend. Numerous observers have noted that online education is here to stay—if only because economies of scale make it relatively cost effective.[4] Thus, it is well worth the trouble of learning how to do it right.

In the Spring of 2020, most instructors had little (if any) preparation for, or knowledge about, how to teach online. This book offers a springboard for the next time courses must be taught online by harvesting decades of knowledge about how students learn and applying this knowledge to remote learning. My goal is to help instructors—from middle school through graduate school—to teach online more successfully, either synchronously (i.e., live, in real time) or asynchronously (i.e., with no fixed meeting times, self-paced or partially self-paced). This book is for both novice and highly experienced online instructors who are not steeped in the science of learning; this book will give you, the instructor, tools that will help students learn more deeply, more easily, and to have fun while doing so.

For students, active learning is far more interesting and effective than simply listening to a lecture. The jury is no longer out about active learning—without question, it is an effective way to learn. But don't take my word for this; here are conclusions from an analysis of 225 studies that compared active learning to traditional teaching methods:

> ❝ The studies analyzed here document that active learning leads to increases in examination performance that would raise average grades by a half a letter, and that failure rates under traditional lecturing increase by 55% over the rates observed under active learning.... Finally, the data suggest that STEM [i.e., Science, Technology, Engineering, and Math] instructors may begin to question the continued use of traditional lecturing in everyday practice, especially in light of recent work indicating that active learning confers disproportionate benefits for STEM students from disadvantaged backgrounds and for female students in male-dominated fields... ❞ [5]

Researchers and commentators quickly seized on the implications of these conclusions. For example, Eric Mazur, a Harvard professor of physics who has been at the forefront of educational innovation (and was not involved in the study) said: "This is a really important article—the impression I get is that it's

---

4   Frank, R. H. (2020, June 5). Don't kid yourself: Online lectures are here to stay. *New York Times*: https://www.nytimes.com/2020/06/05/business/online-learning-winner-coronavirus.html

5   Freeman, S., Eddy, S. L., McDonough, M., Smith, M. K., Okoroafor, N., Jordt, H., & Wenderoth, M. P. (2014). Active learning increases student performance in science, engineering, and mathematics. *Proceedings of the National Academy of Sciences*, 111, 8410-8415. See also Wieman, C. E. (2014). Large-scale comparison of science teaching methods sends clear message. *Proceedings of the National Academy of Sciences, 111*, 8319-8320; Wieman, C. (2017). *Improving how universities teach science: Lessons from the science education initiative*. Cambridge, MA: Harvard University Press.

almost unethical to be lecturing if you have this data."[6] Although I don't share this impression, the point remains that active learning is highly effective. And additional research has documented that the advantages of active learning are not restricted to STEM fields; active learning leads to better outcomes, across the board.[7] Active learning improves how well students understand material, remember it, and know how to apply it across a wide range of situations.

But what exactly is "active learning"? In a nutshell, active learning occurs when a person uses information in the service of achieving a learning outcome. In the classroom context, an instructor has clearly defined learning objectives (intentions of what the students should learn) that lead to specific learning outcomes (the actual learning that is achieved). You, as the instructor, need to design an activity to engage students in material that will help them achieve at least one learning outcome. Active learning is not just "learning by doing." The activity needs to have been designed with a specific point in mind, and students need to be engaged in the activity.[8]

Perhaps counterintuitively, active learning can be effective even if students are not trying to learn: The principles that underlie learning can be at work even if students are not aware of them and even if students are not intentionally trying to achieve a specific learning outcome. The key is to design the activity appropriately (in accordance with the principles described in this book) and to ensure that students are engaged in an activity that helps them to learn the knowledge or skills that are at the heart of a learning outcome. As part of this process, students should understand the purpose of the exercise, which will focus them on the relevant aspects of what they are doing.

Active learning can be entirely self-directed, as might occur when you use YouTube to figure out how to get your toilet to flush properly, when you experiment in the kitchen to learn how to cook a new dish or when you do

---

6   Barak, A. (2014). Lectures aren't just boring they're ineffective, too, study finds. *Science*. https://www.sciencemag.org/news/2014/05/lectures-arent-just-boring-theyre-ineffective-too-study-finds

7   Ambrose, S.A., Bridges, M.W., DiPietro, M., Lovett, M.C., Norman, M.K., & Mayer, R.E. (2010). *How learning works: Seven research-based principles for smart teaching*. San Francisco: Jossey-Bass; Bonwell, C. C., & Eison, J.A. (1991). *Active learning: Creating excitement in the classroom*. ASHE-ERIC Higher Education Report No. 1, Washington, D.C.: The George Washington University, School of Education and Human Development; Mello, D., & Less, C. A. (2013). Effectiveness of active learning in the arts and sciences. *Johnson & Wales University: Humanities Department Faculty Publications & Research. Paper 45*. http://scholarsarchive.jwu.edu/humanities_fac/45; Teagle Foundation (2016). Promoting active learning in the humanities. http://www.teaglefoundation.org/Impacts-Outcomes/Project-Profile/Profiles/Creating-Sustained-Change-in-Practices-of-Engaged

8   For similar, but not identical treatments, see Bonwell, C. C., & Eison, J.A. (1991). *Active learning: Creating excitement in the classroom*. ASHE-ERIC Higher Education Report No. 1, Washington, D.C.: The George Washington University, School of Education and Human Development; "Active Learning" in *Wikipedia*; https://en.wikipedia.org/wiki/Active_learning

research about a particular Civil War battle in order to re-enact it. Although the principles I review in this book apply equally well to such self-directed learning as to instructor-led learning, we will focus on the latter here—in particular, we will focus on how you, as an instructor, can use active learning to make your online classes more effective, engaging and enjoyable.

Most instructors already use some active learning, if only by posing reflection questions, presenting polls, or requiring students to take quizzes. This is a start, but does not take full advantage of what can be accomplished by active learning. Similarly, many instructors sometimes have students break into small groups to discuss an article, case study or issue. Although such group discussions can be helpful, the quality will vary and the focus may be shaky and may veer off-topic. To take full advantage of active learning, the instructor needs a well-defined learning objective and must structure the activity so that students will achieve it.

Here's an example of how to use active learning in a synchronous classroom (e.g., on Google Meet, Webex or Zoom): Let's say that the learning objective is to identify the pluses and minuses of a proposed new law that would fund all elections publicly. One way to use active learning to help students achieve the learning outcome would be to organize a debate, where the "pro" side must formulate arguments in favor and the "con" side must formulate arguments against. One sequence of events that would support this sort of active learning is as follows:

1. You use a spreadsheet to set up numerous small breakout groups (which is easy to do online), with four or five students in each; these groups meet separately to build the best case they can for both sides of the debate—they know that they soon will be assigned to argue either the pro or the con side, but do not know in advance which side they will be assigned. The mere fact of preparing for a debate is a form of active learning. In this scenario, the clearly defined learning objective is to understand a proposed new law on public funding of elections. The students are engaged in an interactive activity, which is listing arguments on both sides.

2. Creating interactive exercises is a good start, but you shouldn't stop there. The students need a way to assess how well they did and to refine and augment their arguments. One way to do this at scale (which does not require you to work overtime to meet the demand) is actually easier to do online than in person. You pair up the groups (e.g., by asking the members of half of the groups to join specific other groups, which you can do easily in Zoom) after they have formulated their arguments, and then ask each of the pairs to compare their notes and help each other by identifying weaknesses in the arguments and sharing additional possible points that could be raised on one side or the other.

Because students are responsible for helping each other, they are led to reflect on the material and think it through.

3. As a third stage you now put the students back in their original groups (by using the spreadsheet you used at the outset), and pair each of these groups with another group (not the one just paired for the evaluation and refinement exercise). You then randomly assign one group of each pair to the "pro" side and one to the "con" side. The pairs of groups then debate, evolving their positions as the debate ensues. You ask them to keep notes on the arguments made by the other side and to record any new arguments that occur to them for either side.

4. Finally, you bring the class together and give each student a list of arguments, asking them individually to write down good counter-arguments. This exercise requires more than just having memorized arguments—it requires deep understanding and analysis. (You might send different sets of arguments to different students, which discourages cheating.) To keep students motivated, you grade these and provide feedback. Critically, all students know from the outset that this will be coming—and hence are motivated to learn as much as they can. The exercise can be set up using "cooperative learning" techniques, for example by rewarding the group as a whole if all members score over a certain amount.[9]

Figure 1.1 Synchronous Debate

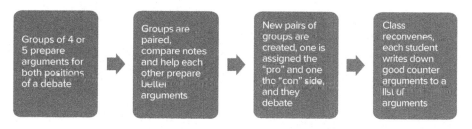

This example shows how active learning occurs when faculty have clearly defined learning objectives; without those learning objectives (in this case, deeply understanding the arguments for the different positions), nothing else would follow. Given such learning objectives, it is possible to design an activity to engage students in material that will help them achieve that goal.

---

9 Slavin, R. E. (2014). Making cooperative learning powerful. *Educational Leadership*, 72, 22-26, Slavin, R. E. (1995). *Cooperative learning: Theory, research, and practice (2nd ed.)*. Boston: Allyn and Bacon.

This example also illustrates something else about active learning: Although it should be stimulating and fun for students, it also often requires them to do more work than if they were just sitting passively listening to a lecture. This is important because researchers have found that students may misinterpret the extra effort required in active learning as indicating that they don't learn as much as they would have learned from a lecture—even when the opposite is in fact true.[10] However, these same researchers found that well over half of the students came to appreciate the effectiveness of active learning as the semester progressed. This feeling can be enhanced by regularly assessing their knowledge and giving them feedback about how much they are learning. These researchers also found that students appreciated active learning more when the instructor preemptively struck, telling them at the outset that they will be working harder but that this signals more, not less, actual learning.

Should Lectures Be Banned?

Active learning is often described as the polar opposite of lectures, where a professor (the "sage on the stage") reads lecture notes and students copy them down. Lectures of this sort are typically characterized as a "continuous exposition by the teacher" (which was the definition used in the analysis that opened this chapter, cited in Note 2). I've heard such lectures dismissively described as "The process whereby the professor's notes are transferred to a student's notes without ever having passed through either of their brains." This perspective has led some to wonder whether instructors should continue to deliver lectures.

However, this characterization of the nature of a lecture is a cartoon, and it makes no sense to dismiss an age-old practice as entirely bad. Rather than simply dismissing the idea of a lecture altogether, we are better off asking, "When and how should a lecture be used?". Wise and experienced scholars have considered this question, and here are consensus views of the major strengths and weaknesses of lectures—all of which apply equally well online as in traditional classroom settings:

Strengths:
- Lectures can boil down the subject matter, putting what's important clearly in the foreground and other material in the background.

- Lecturers can provide novel ways to organize material and make connections that otherwise may not be apparent.

---

10 Deslauriers, L., McCarty, L. S., Miller, K., Callaghan, K., & Kestin, G. (2019). Measuring actual learning versus feeling of learning in response to being actively engaged in the classroom. *Proceedings of the National Academy of Sciences, 116*, 19251-19257.

- Lecturers can tailor their presentations so that they speak to the specific needs, interests and backgrounds of their students.

- Lecturers can make material come alive by injecting enthusiasm and excitement into the presentation.

- Lectures scale: It is as easy to lecture to 1,000 people as it is to lecture to 10 people.

- Lecturers, at their best, can show what it's like to think about problems as an expert, imparting personal knowledge and wisdom.

- If lecturers avoid "cold calling" they can create a "safe space" for students.

- Just like an actor or a comedian, a skilled lecturer can feel the mood of the room and adjust their delivery accordingly.

Weaknesses:

- Not all lecturers are effective at creating or presenting engaging lectures. (In contrast, anyone who knows the field and puts in some effort can succeed at using active learning.)

- Even when students are invited to ask questions, there isn't much feedback for the professor—which impairs their adjusting the pace, depth, and range of the material appropriately.

- Some material doesn't lend itself to being organized into lectures.

- Students typically listen passively and simply write down what they hear or take notes, and hence are less likely to learn.

- Lectures are pitched at a specific level, which may be too easy for some students (and hence boring) and too difficult for other students (and hence frustrating).

- Lectures rest on fixed assumptions about student prior knowledge and can be difficult to adapt on the fly when the assumptions prove incorrect.

- Lectures often are cumulative, and if students miss anything early in the sequence, they then can easily become lost.

- Lectures are often redundant with readings, and thus students feel that attending lectures is a waste of time (they can get the same information in the readings, which they can read at their own pace, review and revisit as desired—and lecture notes are often posted online, which enables students to skip class or busy themselves on their phones during class).

Perhaps the greatest weakness of lectures—and a strong argument for active learning—is that the material often doesn't stick: students may very quickly forget what they heard in a lecture. The most extreme evidence for this that I've found is truly shocking: Researchers reported that students could recall less than 10% of a lecture when tested just three days after hearing it.[11] However, the precise amount that students retain following traditional methods depends on various factors, such as the specific content and level of the course. Other studies report as much 65% retention 18 months after learning physics with traditional methods—but this was still inferior to an active learning group, which retained fully 88% after six months.[12] Another study tested fourth-year pharmacy school students on their retention of material taught earlier in the program, and reported an average of 52% retention for material taught with traditional methods, compared to 60% retention for material taught with active learning.[13] Active learning has consistently been shown to significantly increase the amount that students retain over time compared to traditional lecturing.[14]

Why may students retain relatively little from lectures? One common explanation is that students simply don't pay attention. Although this may sometimes be the case, one myth is worth dispelling: It is not true that students can only pay attention for 10–15 minutes, as has often been claimed.[15] The absurdity of this claim should have been obvious from the mere fact that even young people regularly enjoy hour-long TV shows or much longer movies. However, in the course of investigating just how long students can pay attention, researchers have reported some interesting and useful observations. For example, in one study[16] researchers asked students to click a remote-control device every time they noticed that their attention had drifted from a lecture. The device had three buttons, which

---

11 Bligh, D. (2000). *What's the use of lectures?* New York: Jossey-Bass.

12 Deslauriers, L., & Wieman, C. (2011). Learning and retention of quantum concepts with different teaching methods. *Physical Review Special Topics-Physics Education*, 7:010101. (DOI: 10.1103/PhysRevSTPER.7.010101).

13 Lucas, K. H., Testman, J. A., Hoyland, M. N., Kimble, A. M., & Euler, M. L. (2013). Correlation between active-learning coursework and student retention of core content during advanced pharmacy practice experiences. *American Journal of Pharmaceutical Education, 77*, 171. https://doi.org/10.5688/ajpe778171

14 See also Bonwell, C. C., & Eison, J.A. (1991). *Active learning: Creating excitement in the classroom.* ASHE-ERIC Higher Education Report No. 1, Washington, D.C.: The George Washington University, School of Education and Human Development.

15 Wilson, K., & Korn, J. H. (2007). Attention during lectures: Beyond ten minutes. *Teaching of Psychology, 34*, 85-89; Bradbury, N. A. (2016). Attention span during lectures: 8 seconds, 10 minutes, or more? *Advances in Physiology Education, 40*, 509-513.

16 Bunce, D.M., Flens, E.A., & Nelles, K.Y. (2010). How long can students pay attention in class? A study of student attention decline using clickers. *Journal of Chemical Education, 87*, 1438–1443.

indicated different lengths of time that the student had drifted off (ranging from up to one minute to five minutes or more). The results were clear: Most lapses of attention were for only a minute or less, and the shifts in attention were much more frequent than previously thought (it was not the case that students fell off an attentional cliff after 15 minutes, never to perk up again during that lecture). Although it was true that the lapses became more frequent as the lecture progressed, these lapses were transient—students did tune back in.

So, to return to the question: Why may students retain relatively little from lectures? Lectures typically don't make the most of the principles from the science of learning. The principles summarized later in this book can be applied to lectures as well as to active-learning exercises, but they rarely are. For whatever reason, most of the science of learning has not been readily accessible and explained in a way that any instructor can use—particularly in online courses. I aim to rectify that problem with this book.

In the best of all worlds, students could benefit from the strengths of lectures without falling prey to their weaknesses and instructors could use active learning in combination with lectures to fill in for those weaknesses. Lectures should be used to convey and organize material, to make connections that may otherwise not be apparent, and to motivate students to be interested in the material. Good lectures should be structured so that students can take everything in. They should provide anchoring points and key linkages. The material should be organized to highlight what's most important, and material should be included that speaks to the particular students—taking into account their goals and backgrounds (e.g., level of prior knowledge).

But, that said, lectures should not purely be instructors conveying information and students writing it down. Rather, lectures are more effective if they are punctuated with active learning.[17] This is easy to do online. Moreover, adding active learning can also provide you with the kind of feedback that's difficult to obtain during a lecture, which can help you to teach effectively.

The "Learning Sandwich": Synchronous and Asynchronous Settings

To take advantage of the strengths of lectures, and sidestep their weaknesses, an emerging best practice is to organize a class session into a series of "Learning Sandwiches." The Learning Sandwich takes advantage of the research finding

---

17   Zakrajsek T. (2018). Reframing the lecture versus active learning debate: Suggestions for a new way forward. *Education in the Health Professions* [serial online; cited 20 August 2020]; 1:1-3. http://www.ehpjournal.com/text.asp?2018/1/1/1/242551

that changing pedagogies within a session can keep students engaged—in both synchronous (live) and asynchronous (recorded) online settings. The Learning Sandwich also creates clear structure, which is especially important when students are taking courses online and can be easily distracted. Consider first the Learning Sandwich for synchronous classes:

1. The instructor starts by explaining, illustrating or demonstrating material in a relatively brief lecture. This initial part of the Learning Sandwich should convey a key piece of knowledge (e.g., a concept or fact) or key component of a skill. A live lecture is better than a pre-recorded one in part because it can easily be punctuated every few minutes to keep the students engaged; for example, you might ask students to respond to a poll and then call on some of them to explain why they responded as they did. In fact, research has shown that when something breaks up a lecture— such as a demonstration, question or interesting new slide—students perk up and pay attention. The researchers observed: "This research demonstrates that the positive effect of student-centered pedagogies does more than decrease student inattention during their duration but also has the added benefit of a carryover effect to a subsequent lecture segment. This supports the idea that changing pedagogies within a class period can not only be seen as a way to present concepts in an alternate format but may also help engage students in subsequent lecture teaching formats."[18]

   Alternatively, this first part of the Learning Sandwich can be very brief, simply framing a problem or issue that the students will explore in the next phase.

2. Following the introductory phase, the students should engage in an active-learning exercise that leads them to use the information in some way in the service of achieving a learning outcome. Active learning can be done in a single exercise or a series of related exercises, as illustrated earlier. Active learning is especially easy to implement online when students are in small groups, which provide opportunities for a lot of social interaction. Social interaction should play a central role in formal education for many reasons: For one, students can help each other learn, in multiple ways: Other students can provide "reality checks" that help students calibrate expectations and stay grounded; they can help students overcome conceptual bugs and roadblocks; they can provide the emotional support that keeps students going. Another virtue of small groups is

---

18   Bunce, D.M., Flens, E.A., & Nelles, K.Y. (2010). How long can students pay attention in class? A study of student attention decline using clickers. *Journal of Chemical Education, 87*, 1438–1443. (p, 1142)

that the social dynamics reduce the "free rider" phenomenon, where some students might be tempted to hold back and let others do the work. Moreover, as we shall see, active learning can be personalized "at scale" by creating groups of students who have comparable relevant knowledge or skills, so that no students are bored because it's too easy or frustrated because it's too hard. (However, not all groups should be homogenous in this way, as we consider in the next chapter.) In addition, and crucially, social interactions engender a "feeling of belonging," which can be a buffer against adversities that derail student progress; in fact, the feeling of belonging predicts whether students will continue with their studies.[19] The feeling of belonging can also enhance a student's academic achievement and can even improve their health.

These reasons are why I've emphasized using social active learning exercises throughout this book. It is true that polls and quizzes are forms of active learning, but they are just a sliver of what can be done when students interact with each other.

3. Finally, after breakout groups have ended, the students should be debriefed. A common problem is that students do work in breakout groups but then don't receive feedback about the quality of their performance. The debriefing process can begin by asking students to explain what constitutes an ideal work product. If the class is small enough, you then can call on individual students or groups to present their work product and receive feedback. If the class is large, an alternative way to provide feedback is to give students rubrics to evaluate each other. (Your Learning Management System [LMS] probably allows you to create and use rubrics easily.) At this point, the original groups can pair up again and evaluate each other, using the rubric. You then reconvene the class as a whole and asks groups to indicate what were the common problems.

For example, if the learning outcome were to have students learn one of the principles from the science of learning, you could first explain it (in the opening phase) and then move to active learning. In this case, you might have students devise a brief lesson where they (1) give instructions to other students about how to use the principle, and (2) provide an example where the principle is clearly drawn upon. Following this active learning exercise, they could be graded using a rubric like the one in Table 1.1.

This version of the Learning Sandwich is "front loaded," in the sense that the introductory portion is a relatively long lecture (which may

---

19 Carey, K. (2005). *Choosing to improve: Voices from colleges and universities with better graduation rates*. The Education Trust: Washington, DC; Hausmann, L.R.M., Schofield, J.W., & Woods, R.L. (2007). Sense of belonging as a predictor of intentions to persist among African American and White first-year college students *Research in Higher Education, 48*, 803-839.

include videos and demonstrations) and the point of active learning is to master key material from the lecture. Figure 1.2. illustrates a synchronous Learning Sandwich.

Table 1.1 A Rubric Used for Grading

1	2	3	4	5
Instructions: Not clear; ambiguous and difficult to understand.	**Instructions:** Ambiguous or difficult to understand.	**Instructions:** relatively clear, but slightly ambiguous or somewhat difficult to understand.	**Instructions:** Clear; but could be easier to understand.	**Instructions:** Crystal clear; no ambiguity and easy to understand
Principle: Not clearly described; not obviously drawn upon.	**Principle:** Relatively clearly described; not drawn upon.	**Principle:** Clearly described; barely drawn upon.	**Principle:** Clearly described; not drawn upon well.	**Principle:** Very clearly described; drawn upon very well.

Figure 1.2 Synchronous Learning Sandwich

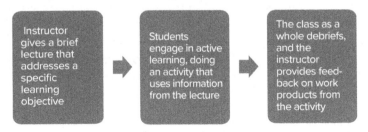

A variant is to have a "back-loaded" Learning Sandwich. In this case the introductory part of the Learning Sandwich does not have a formal lecture, but instead frames a problem or issue that the students then explore in the active learning component; the problem or issue is typically difficult for the students, and they have to struggle to address it—and thus may be particularly motivated to learn the answer. In this back-loaded version, the debrief allows the instructor to convey information, sometimes as a dramatic "reveal" that satisfies the students' curiosity.

Perhaps the best known method that relies on this structure is "Peer Instruction," which is the name Eric Mazur gave to his innovative active-learning technique.[20]

---

20 See Mazur, E. (1997). *Peer instruction: A user's manual.* Saddle River, NJ: Prentice Hall.

To use it, you first must specify learning objectives at a granular level. For each one, you use the first phase of the Learning Sandwich to introduce a puzzle that has several possible answers. For example, if teaching thermodynamics, you might ask students to predict the results of a demonstration; for instance, you could ask students to imagine a sheet of iron that has a circular hole cut out of the center. The sheet is heated up until it is uniformly red hot. The question is: Would that hole stay the same size as before the sheet was heated, shrink, or expand? In the exercise, the class first is asked this question and asked to vote for one of the possible effects.

Following this, in the second phase, the class is organized into small groups to discuss their answers; these groups can be particularly effective if they each include students who disagreed in their votes. You (as the instructor) and teaching assistants dip into breakout groups, listen in, and provide hints (e.g., the fact that the sheet is heated uniformly is critical because all molecules would be pushing against each other to the same degree).

After five minutes or so, the class reconvenes and the third, debrief, phase begins by asking students to vote again. (In general, the answers are more accurate the second time.) Then you provide the correct answer and explain why it is correct. (Incidentally, the correct answer is that the hole expands as the sheet is heated uniformly—the molecules near the hole are expanding outward, like all of the other molecules.)

Figure 1.3 Back-Loaded Learning Sandwich

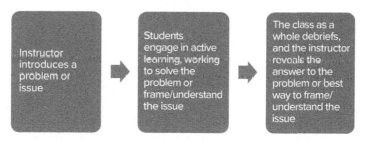

In short, the information transmission component of the Learning Sandwich can be front-loaded, as occurs most commonly (in typical lecture situations) or can be back-loaded, as occurs with peer instruction and various "reveal" methods (where students puzzle over a problem and the answer is then revealed, but without the voting and specific trappings of peer instruction). It is also possible to distribute information transmission over both the introductory and debrief phases.

Each class has a sequence of Learning Sandwiches. An example of a 90-minute class that uses both front-loaded and back-loaded Learning Sandwiches is presented in Table 1.2.

Table 1.2 Class Overview

Duration (Minutes)	Slides	Description
		Learning Sandwich 1 (Back-Loaded)
5	1-6	Intro: Framing the problem + poll
5	7	Single-Phase Breakout Groups
10	8-9	Debrief + poll + Lecture
		Learning Sandwich 2 (Front-Loaded)
10	10-19	Lecture + video
10	20-21	Two-Phase Breakout Groups
5	22-23	Debrief, Q & A
		Learning Sandwich 3 (Front-Loaded)
10	24-29	Lecture + demonstration
15	30-31	Three-Phase Breakout Groups
5	32	Debrief + poll
5	33-35	Wrap Up + Q&A
10	36	Quiz

This same sort of "Learning Sandwich" can be used in asynchronous online settings, on the various platforms that many online instructors are currently working with—such as Canvas, Blackboard, D2L/Brightspace, and Moodle.

1. In an asynchronous setting, the first phase is recorded. This can be an entire lecture or the framing of a problem or issue that the students should address. Asynchronous settings have the major virtues that students can progress at their own pace and can easily go back to review earlier material. (However, in some types of asynchronous instruction students have a well-defined window within which to work, starting and ending on specific dates and times—but even here they can work at their own pace within these confines.)

This method of instruction has the major drawback that there usually isn't much opportunity for students to obtain detailed feedback about how well they are learning and students can easily become stuck, frustrated, unmotivated and simply stop their studies.

To begin to address such problems, you (the instructor) should set up a bulletin board, discussion forum, or shared doc and invite students to ask questions. In general, students should be asked to anchor their questions to a specific elapsed time in a recorded lecture, so that it's very clear to all readers (other students as well as the instructor) exactly what is being asked. To ensure prompt feedback, you should commit to checking for questions and responding to them at least twice a day (but, to be clear, students only post when they have a question; students are not required to check twice a day!).

2. For the second phase, which includes an active learning exercise, you can create working groups by asking each student to indicate on a bulletin board or shared document when they have finished going through the introductory material; the most commonly used asynchronous platforms have designated spaces for students to discuss and respond to posts from their peers (in fact, the discussion forum is the core of many current asynchronous online courses). Given entries in such a doc, you could simply assign the specified number (e.g., four) of contiguous students to the same group. You send the students in each group instructions and, if appropriate, a "model" of an ideal work product or rubric.

    The students then interact either in writing (on a shared doc) or by leaving video clips for other students to access when possible (note: these clips need to be placed in a secure environment, where only the other students in the group and the you—the instructor—can access them).

    A variant of this approach for the second phase in an asynchronous setting is to have students enter their names and email addresses on a bulletin board (or shared doc) when they have finished the introductory material, along with the days and times when they will be available for a video chat. Students then select others based on the convenience of the timing, and the group then interacts in real time at the allotted hour. This is a hybrid model, which combines asynchronous and synchronous components. Nothing very fancy is required for this: Just a collaborative authoring service (e.g., Google Docs) and a video conferencing service (e.g., Google Meet, Webex, Zoom, etc.).

3. And, finally, the debrief component of the Learning Sandwich can be conducted by sending email or video to individual groups and asking them to report back, copying the class as a whole—this is equivalent to calling on a single group at a time. And a hybrid model can also be used to conduct the debrief component live, which gives students a chance to ask questions and have them answered in real time. In some cases, a wrap-up lecture can also be recorded for this final phase of the Learning Sandwich.

This simple idea of the Learning Sandwich has an enormous amount of learning science built into it. The rest of this book unpacks and elaborates the science and ideas underlying these recommendations.

Here's a quick overview of what is to come:

Chapter 2. The Science of Learning: This chapter summarizes key facts about cognitive functioning that provide the foundations for the principles at the core of the book. In particular, it reviews the relationships between "learning" and "memory" and describes several different types of "memory stores" that exist in the human brain. It also discusses factors that affect different phases of learning, from encoding, to storage, to retention, to retrieval of stored information.

Chapter 3. Deep Processing: This is the first of five chapters that summarize the principles from the science of learning.[21] The key idea here is that the more mental processing a person performs on information, the more likely it is that the person later will remember it. This principle lies at the core of all active learning, and thus we begin with it as a foundation. Crucially, mental processing must focus on material that will achieve the learning outcomes, and such processing can be induced by many forms of active learning.

Chapter 4. Chunking: People can only take in about three or four organized units of information ("chunks"). Chunking applies to all forms of information, ranging from perceptual (e.g., visual, auditory) to conceptual. This principle guides not only how instructors should structure their course materials and activities, but also how each class should be organized so that it can function well online.

Chapter 5. Building Associations: Associations play a crucial role in organizing information when it is first encountered, in integrating information into what is already known so that it is retained well, and in providing cues that make information easy to retrieve. Associations help to solve the greatest single problem in the science of learning: the problem of transfer, of applying information learned in class to situations in work and daily life.

---

21 I have organized these principles in the most concise way I could devise, with an eye toward formulating them so that they can be most usefully applied to teaching and learning. Other researchers have proposed alternative organizations—but it is all the same material, just organized differently. For example, see Graesser, A.C., Halpern, D.F., & Hakel, M. (2008). *25 principles of learning.* Washington, DC: Task Force on Lifelong Learning at Work and at Home. (For a summary, see Graesser, A.C., (2009). *Journal of Educational Psychology, 101,* 259-261.); Willingham, D. T. (2009). *Why don't students like school? A cognitive scientist answers questions about how the mind works and what it means for the classroom.* San Francisco, CA: Wiley/Jossey-Bass

Chapter 6. Dual Coding: Learning and memory are more effective when information is presented in multiple modalities, such as visually and verbally: showing and telling is better than either perceptual or verbal modes alone. This principle reflects the fact that our brains have multiple different memory stores, and we learn information better when it can be entered into more than one such store.

Chapter 7. Deliberate Practice: Deliberate practice requires behaving in a specific way, receiving feedback, paying attention to what is different between the initial behavior and the feedback, and using the feedback to refine the behavior. Perhaps counterintuitively, learning is best when students make errors; only after they make errors can they receive the kind of feedback that will best improve learning. This chapter explains how the process of "deliberate practice" works.

Chapter 8. Combining Principles: Although the principles can be drawn on individually, they gain force when they are combined. We here consider a range of practices, from the power of testing to the use of mnemonics to gamification, and see how these practices can be designed to draw on combinations of the principles and thereby enhance learning.

Chapter 9. Intrinsic and Extrinsic Motivation: None of the principles of the science of learning will have any effect unless students participate and are engaged. This chapter discusses ways to motivate students, based both on theories of intrinsic motivation and on theories of extrinsic motivation. We focus on how to bake such motivational factors into online active learning.

Chapter 10. Exercises and Activities: We conclude with many examples of specific types of active learning activities and particular exercises; all of these activities and exercises can be done effectively online, often both in synchronous and in asynchronous settings. Using these examples as a starting place can help you make online education not just "good," but truly superb.

The recommendations I offer here allow you to structure online courses that are fun, friendly, and familiar. The key is in the learning techniques, not the specific online technologies. I have intentionally offered activities that can be implemented on a wide range of platforms in many ways. By the end of this book you should be in a good position to be proud of how you teach an online class; but more than that, you should be able to design and develop activities that help students learn—and enjoy doing so.

—2—

The Science of Learning

When teaching about the science of learning, I sometimes begin by asking a question: At the end of the day, do you ever reflect back on the events of the day? (Please try to answer this yourself.) The vast majority of people I've asked have said that they do this, at least some of the time. I then ask the question I'm really interested in: How much of what you recall in the evening about the events of the day do you think you tried to memorize at the time the event was taking place? I then ask the audience to raise their hands if they think they intentionally memorized at least half of what they later recalled. Nobody has ever raised a hand. I then ask them to raise their hands if they think they intentionally memorized about 25% of what they later recalled. To date, three people (out of well over 1,000) have raised their hands. I then ask them to raise their hands if they intentionally memorized about 20%, then 15%, and so on, reducing the amount in 5% increments. The majority of people consistently raise their hands at the 5% mark.

Even if people are off by half, these responses are remarkable: People often believe that they remember what they have intentionally tried to learn, but in fact they typically do not try to memorize the vast majority of what they later recall at the end of the day. This raises a fundamental question: If they didn't try to learn what happened during the day, how can they remember it later?

In fact, findings in the science of learning lead us to expect exactly this sort of response to my question about how much of what is remembered is intentionally learned. As discussed in the following chapter, a large amount of what we recall is simply a byproduct of paying attention and thinking about the event or material. Memory is often a spin-off of mental processing; it's just something we pick up along the way.

This is only one of many findings from the science of learning, but it illustrates a key point: Much of what has been learned about learning is not intuitively obvious. The situation reminds me of the old saying, "The fish is the last one to find out about water": We are so immersed in our daily lives that we take our mental processes for granted, and rarely pause to consider their workings—even when they are accessible to our consciousness, which they often are not.[22]

The principles of the science of learning are the key to getting the most out of active learning. These principles capture central facts about how the brain functions, and an effective active learning exercise should be informed by these principles. Knowing this, you can design better active learning exercises simply by considering how best to draw on the underlying principles about how the brain learns.

The science of learning is primarily an outgrowth of research on basic cognitive functions, notably those that underlie how we organize information when we first encounter it, how we understand and integrate new information into what we already know, and how we access information we've previously learned. The primary goal of the science of learning is to produce a set of principles that are broad and deep, and that can be applied in a wide range of circumstances. For example, the anecdote above about memory illustrates the "Principle of Deep Processing," which states that "The more mental processing one performs on information, the more likely it is that one will retain that information." The principles that underlie the science of learning have been augmented and fleshed out via studies that focus on identifying and validating specific interventions that improve learning or teaching. For example, researchers have shown that the mere act of taking a test—even if students are not told the correct answers afterwards—actually helps students to learn.[23]

The science of learning is broader than it might seem at first glance: Learning per se is about acquiring new knowledge or skills (in any field or domain of study); it is about taking in something and storing it in the brain's memory banks. But the science of learning isn't just about how we pick up and store new knowledge or

---

22 For example, see Damasio, A. (1994/2005). *Descarte's error: Emotion, reason, and the human brain.* New York: Penguin; Libet, B. (2005). *Mind time: The temporal factor in consciousness.* Cambridge, MA: Harvard University Press.

23 Roediger, H. L., & Karpicke, J. D. (2006). Test-enhanced learning: Taking memory tests improves long-term retention. *Psychological Science, 17,* 249–255.

skills. The science of learning is also about how we organize information (e.g., facts, concepts, procedures) in a way that will make it stick in our memories and about how we later access and use information that we've previously stored. The science of learning is also about how we relate our understanding of something new to what we already know and about how that affects when and why we use what we learn. The breadth of the science of learning makes it applicable to many aspects of teaching. For example, if you learn the details of the Principle of Deep Processing, you should be able to use that information to design numerous aspects of lesson plans; your knowledge of the principle should allow you to apply it in different ways, in different contexts, with different types of materials.

Key Facts about the Brain: Foundations of the Principles

The science of learning hinges on key facts about how the brain works; that's where the principles ultimately come from. Here's a very, very quick (perhaps ridiculously quick) overview of critical things researchers have learned about how the brain learns[24]; we will build on these foundations in the following chapters.

To make this concrete, let's take the case of learning a new concept, say the concept of "sunk costs": When making a decision, think only about future costs—the past is the past and previous costs are done and gone.[25]

To begin, we need to appreciate that learning and memory are so intimately related that it's best to think of them as just different sides of the same coin. When students hear about the concept of "sunk costs," they try to understand and remember it (as we shall see, without understanding it, they will have difficulty remembering it). As noted above, learning is the process whereby we come to acquire and enter new knowledge or skills into our memory banks. In contrast, memory is the result of learning—it is what is stored in these memory banks. Without memory, learning may as well not have occurred. When instructors say that they want students to learn about sunk costs, for example, what they really mean is that they want students to understand, remember and know how to apply that concept appropriately—they want certain information to be stored in memory.

Types of Memories

But true learning isn't just about getting information into any sort of memory bank. It turns out that our brains have more than one kind of memory.[26] Instructors

---

24 If you want more detail, see Smith, E.E., & Kosslyn, S. M. (2006). *Cognitive psychology: Mind and brain*. New York, NY: Prentice Hall.

25 Sunk Cost, in *Wikipedia*: https://en.wikipedia.org/wiki/Sunk_cost

26 For an expanded treatment, see Kosslyn, S. M., & Rosenberg, R. S. (2020). *Introducing psychology: Brain, person, group (5th edition)*. Boston, MA: FlatWorld.

want more than to have students store information about sunk costs in short-term memory[27]; information in *short-term memory* is just what we are consciously aware of knowing. Short-term memories can be retained for only about half a minute, at most, and we can only retain about three or four groups of information—and this is a major bottleneck on what we can learn (which leads directly to the Principle of Chunking, discussed in Chapter 4). If someone tells you a phone number to call right away, you store it in short-term memory between the moment of hearing it and when you finish tapping in the number. In contrast, *long-term memory* contains everything we have learned and now know; all the facts, words, concepts, images, procedures, and so on. If students recall the concept of sunk costs only for a short period of time, the instructor will not be happy.

The process of storing information about sunk costs (or anything else) in long-term memory usually starts with retaining it briefly in short-term memory, after students have heard, read or viewed new information. The goal then is to help students convert what's in their short-term memories to material they store in their long-term memories. That's core to how we want to use the principles of the science of learning: To devise ways to help students tuck information away in a durable form, so they later can recall and use this information.

The brain stores information in long-term memory in multiple ways. As we discuss in Chapter 6, learning is enhanced when people store both words and images. This results in part because every perceptual system (e.g., vision, hearing, and touch) also serves to store those sorts of memories, both short-term and long-term. For example, we have distinct visual long-term memories, which we can recall to produce visual mental images in short-term memory. For instance, please answer this question: What shape are Mickey Mouse's ears? In order to answer, most people recall the cartoon rodent and "look" at the ears in their mental image to see that they are circular. The information was there in long-term memory, but to use it you needed to bring it into short-term memory, and hence become conscious of it.

When we hear or read a description, such as of sunk costs, we typically store the concepts that are conveyed by language—we store the meaning, the "gist," not the specific words. People who speak more than one language may even forget which language was used to describe something; they clearly are storing the meaning, not the words themselves. This is a different type of memory from

---

27 The concept of Working Memory is sometimes now treated as a more modern version of the concept of Short-Term Memory, but it is in fact a broader concept—including processes that operate on what is in memory in addition to the memory store itself. I focus here on the memory store per se; cf. Baddeley, A.D. (2007). *Working memory, thought and action*. Oxford: Oxford University Press; Baddeley, A.D. (2010). Working memory. *Current Biology, 20*, R136-R140.

the perceptual memory of the words as we hear or read them. Most "academic" knowledge is of this type, which draws deeply on language, be it heard (in lectures, in discussions) or read (in textbooks, in articles).

Did you know that there's a type of knowledge that you can't call into consciousness? For instance, do you know how you are able to keep your balance on a bike? All of what has been discussed so far focuses on information that we can bring into short-term memory (as in the Mickey Mouse example), but a lot of what we know we can only access when we are actually using it. The first sort of knowledge is often called *declarative* knowledge, and includes facts, concepts, words, and images. The second sort of information is often called *procedural* knowledge, and includes skills such as your knowledge of how to do arithmetic (of the sort that would be required to figure out the magnitude of financial sunk costs), ride a bike, or how to produce grammatical sentences in your native language.

Procedural memories allow us to perform tasks "automatically," without needing to consciously think about what we are doing.[28] We often begin by learning declarative information about a rule or process but after we use it a lot, it becomes a procedural memory and hence automatic. For example, when first learning a new language you are probably very aware of the specific rules of grammar, but with practice you can form sentences automatically and intuitively. Or when you are first learning to drive a car, you consciously think through every step—but with practice, the knowledge becomes procedural and automatic.

The main reason it is important to keep in mind the distinction between declarative and procedural knowledge is that our limited short-term memory capacity is a major bottleneck in how well we can learn and reason. When you can perform a skill automatically, you remove the burden on short-term memory—freeing it up to do other things.[29] For instance, after you have a lot of practice driving a car, you have no problem carrying on a conversation while steering, braking, watching out for obstacles, and so forth (but having a conversation with a beginner while they're driving is an invitation to have an accident).

Clearly, there is more than one way to learn and remember. As we shall see in Chapter 6, the Principle of Dual Coding capitalizes on this fact by leading instructors to help students learn material in at least two different ways, typically

---

28 Anderson, J. R., Bothell, D., Byrne, M. D., Douglass, S., Lebiere, C., & Qin, Y. (2004). An integrated theory of the mind. *Psychological Review, 111*, 1036-1060; Clark, R. E. (2011). The impact of non-conscious knowledge on educational technology research and design. *Educational Technology, July-August*, 3-11; Squire, L.R. (2004). Memory systems of the brain: A brief history and current perspective. *Neurobiology of Learning and Memory, 82*, 171–177.

29 Sweller, J., Ayres, J., & Kalyuga, S. (2011). *Cognitive load theory*. New York: Springer-Verlag.

verbally and visually. (However, I must note that in spite of this fact, there is no evidence that some of us are "visual learners," others "verbal learners," and so forth—we all can use the different modalities effectively.[30])

Accessing Memories

If a tree falls in a forest and nobody is there to hear it, did it make a sound? Cognitive scientists have a definitive answer to this old chestnut: The answer is No. We distinguish between the physical event, waves in a medium (the air, water, etc.) and the brain's response to those waves. If no brain registers the waves, there was no "sound." Similarly to the tree falling and creating waves in the air that never reach an ear, if stored information cannot affect behavior, it may as well not exist.

Procedural memories are typically accessed by the appropriate "trigger" conditions. You access your knowledge of how to drive when you are behind the wheel of a car; you use the rules of grammar when you are speaking a language. In contrast, accessing declarative memories is more complicated, and this is what we will focus on because most formal learning is about acquiring such information (e.g., facts, concepts, images).

Declarative memories aren't stored like neatly alphabetized files in a filing cabinet. Rather, they are cross-referenced directly and indirectly, via other stored information. We don't just recall that birds have feathers; we also know that they are animals (and hence eat and breathe), that they have a distant relationship with dinosaurs, and perhaps that they have hollow bones. Everything we know fits into a web of knowledge and belief in our long-term memories. As we shall see in Chapter 5 when we consider the Principle of Associations, such a rich mass of associations plays a crucial role in how we can best organize information in order to enter it into long-term memory, how we retain information securely in long-term memory over time, and how we later access that information when we want to use it. Managing to sock away in memory the concept of sunk costs won't do students any good if they cannot later use this information when they make decisions.

Additional key facts about learning in the brain are relevant to how we assess what students have learned, which requires devising ways to have them demonstrate their knowledge. All forms of assessments fall into one of two categories, which tap different mental processes. On the one hand, students can be asked to *recall* the information, which requires digging it out of long-

---

30 See Pashler, H., McDaniel, M., Rohrer, D., & Bjork, R. (2008). Learning styles: Concepts and evidence. *Psychological Science in the Public Interest, 9*, 105-119; Willingham, D. T. (2009). *Why don't students like school? A cognitive scientist answers questions about how the mind works and what it means for the classroom.* San Francisco, CA: Wiley/Jossey-Bass

term memory and activating it in short-term memory so that they are aware of it—which in turn allows them to create a product of some kind. For example, asking students to write down a description of a concept, such as sunk costs, requires them to recall that information. So does asking them to draw a sketch of a fountain they saw, to summarize key facts about a Civil War battle, or to write computer code to sort a list. In all cases, students are able to produce something based on information they have retrieved from their long-term memories.

On the other hand, rather than asking students to recall information, you can ask them to *recognize* it. In this case, you would ask them to pick out the correct alternative from a set of choices or to decide whether a claim or description is correct. To recognize the correct answer, students need to match the choices to what they previously stored in long-term memory; if students didn't store the information effectively, they will have trouble later recognizing it. Multiple-choice and True/False tests are the classic ways to use recognition to assess what students know.

This distinction between recall and recognition is important in part because we can use recognition to give us feedback even when we cannot recall perfectly—which can help us to learn new things. This fact is critical to the Principle of Deliberate Practice, which we consider in Chapter 7.

Transfer

Finally, people tend not to use information outside of the narrow context where they learned it. This is a problem because the goal of teaching about sunk costs (or anything else) is not simply to allow students to recall or recognize definitions or the like. Rather, instructors want students to use what they learn in class when they later make decisions and solve problems at work and in their daily lives. Achieving this goal requires students to transfer what they learn from one context to another.

Consider this anecdote a colleague told me: His friend was asked to teach physics to non-majors. He decided that to make it interesting, he should use a lot of examples from baseball. (There's a lot of physics in baseball, such as Newton's Third Law at work when a bat hits a ball.) The problem was that he used so many baseball examples in his lectures that he ran out of them by the time of the final exam. So, instead he used football examples for the final exam. The result? The students rebelled! The common sentiment ran along the lines of "The whole class was about baseball and then you tricked us in the final, switching to football! This isn't fair!!" This was a clear example of a failure to transfer, but in this case this is a failure of near transfer—the original situation was similar to the new one, and they weren't separated much in time. In contrast, far transfer involves transferring knowledge or skills from one situation to another that seems dissimilar (e.g., learning about the solar system and applying that to the atom) and the situations are often separated in time.[31]

To teach effectively, the methods of instruction should be designed to encourage transfer. Nobody—not teachers, students, or administrators—wants to teach material that stays in the classroom and is never used by the students outside of class.

Transfer can be encouraged by three practices:

1. Instructors should give students a wide range of concrete examples and should explain in detail how they are related. The goal is to help students later easily bring to mind phrases such as "It reminds me of...", "It's like...", and "It's the same as..." when they encounter related situations or material.[32]

2. Instructors should help students achieve learning outcomes that correspond as closely as possible to what students actually want to do at work or in their daily lives. Thus, the learning objectives should be specific and concrete. For example, if the instructor wants to teach students to be critical consumers of news, the learning objectives should help the students learn specific actions such as considering whether a news source might be biased.

3. Instructors should design the activities themselves to be as close as possible to what students actually do outside of class. For example, if the goal is to teach negotiation skills, a role-playing activity that mimics actual negotiations is better than a problem-solving activity where students try to determine the best approach.

This brief overview provides the foundation for most of the principles to be discussed in the following chapters; I will add additional background when we need it. In many cases, hundreds (if not thousands) of studies underlie each of the principles in the science of learning. The scientific literature has been accumulating for well over 100 years, and it is remarkable that so little of it has been used systematically in teaching. I hope that you the reader will help to change that by using what is presented in the following chapters.

---

31 Barnett, S., & Ceci, S. (2002). When and where do we apply what we learn? A taxonomy for far transfer. *Psychological Bulletin 128*, 612-637.

32 Haskell, R. E. (2000). *Transfer of learning: Cognition, instruction, and reasoning.* New York: Academic Press; Kober, N. (2015). *Reaching students: What research says about effective instruction in undergraduate science and engineering.* Board on Science Education, Division of Behavioral and Social Sciences and Education. Washington, DC: The National Academies Press.

—3—

Deep Processing

My favorite experiment in all of cognitive psychology was carried out by Gordon Bower in 1970.[33] Here's what he did: He asked participants to listen to pairs of words such as "cow-tree," "fork-guitar," and "bag-rock." The participants were organized into three groups, which received the same list of pairs of words but had different instructions about what to do with them. One group was told to say the pairs of words silently to themselves, over and over, and try to memorize which words went together. A second group was told to visualize the named objects interacting in some way (e.g., a cow rubbing against a tree, a guitar with a fork stuck into it), and try to memorize which words went together. And a third group was told simply to visualize the named objects interacting in some way, and then to rate how vivid the mental image seemed to be (ranging from very dim and vague to very sharp and realistic). This last group was not told anything about trying to memorize the pairs of words and was not warned of an impending memory test.

All three groups then received a memory test where they got the first word of each pair (e.g., "cow," "fork" and "bag") and were supposed to recall the other word in that pair. The results were straightforward: First, the second group, which visualized the objects interacting and tried to memorize them, later recalled about twice as much as the first group, which silently verbalized the names and tried to memorize them. Second, the most interesting finding, in my view, was that the third group—which visualized the objects interacting but did not try to memorize them—did as well as the second group even though the memory test

---

33 Bower, G. H. (1972). Mental imagery and associative learning. In L. Gregg (Ed.), *Cognition in learning and memory* (pp. 51-88). New York: John Wiley & Sons.

was a surprise, and did about twice as well as the first group (which, unlike the third group, intentionally tried to memorize the word pairs).

This finding is remarkable: The mere act of creating the mental images and "looking at them" to rate their vividness was enough to lodge the associations in memory—even though the participants were not trying to memorize the words. This is very much along the lines of the sorts of memories you have of events that took place earlier that day, the vast majority of which you probably did not try to memorize at the time they occurred.

These kinds of phenomena illustrate the Principle of Deep Processing, which states that "The more mental processing one performs on information, the more likely it is that one will retain that information."[34] By "information" I mean knowledge (e.g., facts, concepts, words, images) and skills (specific types of procedures that are used to achieve specific goals).

The Principle of Deep Processing lies at the core of why active learning works; it is the central principle that underlies why active learning is better than passive learning (e.g., listening to a lecture). The other principles either set the stage for engaging in specific types of deep processing or augment this principle in some way.

I have often demonstrated this principle in large groups. Pretend that you are a participant, and get a sense for what it's like to do these tasks.

1. First, I ask the people in the room to pair up, starting from the left of each row. I then tell them that the person on the left of each pair (from their point of view) will have different instructions than the person on the right. Specifically: I ask the person on the left of each pair to look at each word in a list about to be shown, and silently decide whether or not it names a living thing (e.g., "tree" does, "rock" does not). In contrast, I ask the person on the right of each pair to look at the same list, but now to silently decide whether the first letter of each word ascends higher than the letter at the end of the word (e.g., the "h" in "house" ascends higher than the "e", but the "m" in "most" does not ascend higher than the "t").

2. Second, I show the following list:

frog

harp

---

34 For a different treatment of this principle, see Kosslyn, S.M. (2017). The science of learning. In S. M. Kosslyn & B. Nelson. (Eds.) *Building the intentional university*. Cambridge, MA: MIT Press. See also Craik, F. I. M., & Lockhart, R. S. (1972). Levels of processing: A framework for memory research. *Journal of Verbal Learning and Verbal Behavior, 11,* 671-684; Craig, S. D., Sullins, J., Witherspoon, A., & Gholson, B. (2006). The deep-level reasoning effect: The role of dialogue and deep-level-reasoning questions during vicarious learning. *Cognition and Instruction, 24,* 565-591.

rat

sheet

deer

brick

rug

bear

forge

hare

stone

ape

lamp

snail

chair

worm

Playing the role of the person on the left of a pair, take a look at that first word—does it name a living thing? (Yes). The second word? (No) The third? (Yes). And so on. Now play the role of the person on the right: Does the first letter of the first word ascend higher than the last letter? (Yes) And the first letter of the second word? (Yes). The first letter of the third word? (No). You get the idea.

I ask the participants to raise their hands when they have gone through the entire list, and I remove the list when everyone has raised their hands.

1. Fifteen seconds later, without prior warning, I ask the participants to recall as many words that were on the list as they could. (This was often met with groans.) They have 20 seconds to write down the words or just bring them to mind.

2. Following this, I show the list again and ask the participants to count how many words they correctly recalled. (And I tell them that they are on the Honor System!)

3. And, finally, I ask each person to compare the number they got right with the number their partner got right—and to raise their hands if the person on the left of the pair (who judged living/non-living) got more correct.

The typical result: The vast majority of people who were on the left (who judged living/non-living) got more correct than the people on the right (who judged relative letter height). Why? Judging whether a word names a living thing requires more mental processing than judging surface properties. To decide whether a named object is living, you probably need to think about characteristics such as whether it moves of its own volition or is a plant; but to decide which letter is higher, you just need to look at what you were given, with no need to dig into memory before being able to make the decision. The more you process information mentally, the more likely you are to recall it later—even if you aren't trying to learn it.

Targeted Processing

To use deep processing when designing active learning exercises online, it's crucial to be aware of one key fact: You need to ensure that students are processing deeply the relevant and appropriate information. For example, consider the implications of one classic study:[35] Participants began either by judging an aspect of the meaning of words or by judging whether words rhyme with another particular word. Following this, the participants were given a memory test, and half of the people in each of the two groups were led to focus on the meanings of the words and half were led to focus on the sounds of the words.

The important finding: Participants who initially judged the meanings of words later could recall words better when focusing on their meanings than when focusing on how they sounded. But exactly the opposite was found when participants initially judged how words sounded. In this case, they later were better at remembering words with specific sounds than words that had specific meanings.

The point is that more mental processing results in better memory for what was processed. It's not that one sort of judgment or type of processing always leads to better learning, and it's not the sheer amount of mental processing that's important. Rather, what is important is the amount of processing of the relevant information. This point is not just about memorizing words; it applies more generally to learning knowledge or skills.[36] You get what you teach.

---

35 Morris, D. C., Bransford, J. D., & Franks, J. J. (1977). Levels of processing versus transfer appropriate processing. *Journal of Verbal Learning and Verbal Behavior, 16*, 519-533.

36 Berry, J.W., & Chew, S.L., (2008). Improving learning through interventions of student-generated questions and concept maps. *Teaching of Psychology, 35*, 305-312; Chew, S.L. (2005). Seldom in doubt but often wrong: Addressing tenacious student misconceptions. In D.S. Dunn, & S.L. Chew, (Eds.), *Best practices in teaching general psychology* (pp. 211-223). Mahwah, NJ: Erlbaum; Nolen, S. B. (1988). Reasons for studying: Motivational orientations and study strategies. *Cognition and Instruction, 5*, 269-287.

You can lead students to deeply process the relevant information by how you structure the activity. Here's an example of one way to do this that is relatively easy to do online, but difficult to use in a traditional classroom.

Let's go back to the example of a learning objective from Chapter 1, where we want students to understand the pluses and minuses of a proposed new law that would fund all elections publicly. We can use a debate as a form of active learning, but now let me use this to illustrate a variant of a particularly powerful technique called a "jigsaw classroom".[37] In a jigsaw classroom students meet in two sets of breakout groups, one after the other. In the first set, each group prepares one part of a multipart project or activity. After a fixed amount of time, these groups are broken up and reassembled into new groups (this is the "jigsaw" part), where each new group has at least one representative (depending on the specific activity) from each type of the initial groups. This technique can be used in many ways, and can easily focus students on a specific learning objective. For example:.

1. You, as the instructor, begin by organizing students into breakout groups, each of which has six students. You define two types of groups; students in one type prepare for the "pro" side whereas students in the other prepare for the "con" side. You can set up these breakout groups in advance (e.g., by using a spreadsheet).[38]

2. After a fixed amount of time (e.g., 10 minutes), you break up each group and create new groups; each new group contains three students from one of the previous "pro" groups and three students from one of the previous "con" groups. (You can do this easily in Zoom by showing students a spreadsheet that assigns each of them to a specific new breakout room, and ask them simply to move to that room.)

3. The six students in each of these new groups then debate the issue, and each side tries to convince the other and—at the same time   tries to identify the strongest and weakest arguments of their opponents.

4. Following the debate, the students individually have five minutes to write down what they thought were their strongest and weakest arguments and their opponents' strongest and weakest arguments, with a brief justification of their evaluations. They would be told at the outset that they will be graded on this, which would motivate them to pay attention. Crucially, you should provide specific feedback that addresses how well students achieved the learning outcome.[39]

---

37 See: https://en.wikipedia.org/wiki/Jigsaw_learning_technique; https://en.wikipedia.org/wiki/Jigsaw_(teaching_technique)

38 For example, see https://blog.zoom.us/using-zoom-breakout-rooms/

39 Kluger, A. N., & DeNisi, A. (1998). Feedback interventions: Toward the understanding of a double-edged sword. *Current Directions in Psychological Science, 7*, 67–72

This jigsaw exercise both invokes deep processing and focuses students specifically on what you want them to learn.

Teaching online allows us to extend the jigsaw technique in various ways. For example, you could use a multistep role-playing activity where each group is aligned with a different stakeholder. Say that you want to teach negotiation skills.[40] You first need to describe such skills and explain how to use them effectively; for example, you might teach the students specific tactics, such as presenting a very high initial request to "anchor" the negotiation, with an eye toward inching down as necessary—but you would explain that they need to be careful that this request isn't so high as to be unreasonable, which would sour the negotiation. These concepts are not rocket science and most people can easily understand them, but they may be difficult to apply in practice—which is why you would devote time to active learning in breakout groups.

Figure 3.1 Jigsaw Debate

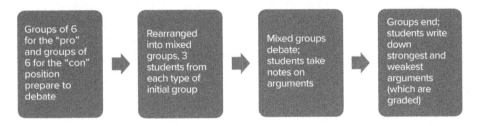

A role-playing simulation is a good way to use active learning to teach negotiation skills; role playing is particularly compatible with negotiations among distinct stakeholders (and hence supports transfer to the actual activity). For example, your learning objectives could be to teach eight negotiation tactics and how to use them effectively. To this end, you could create a role-playing simulation of how a school district selects new computers. (Students will understand why the stakeholders care about getting new computers.) You could specify the stakeholders as the faculty (who will press to obtain high-powered machines), the tech staff (who will push for easy-to-maintain models), the administrators (who will urge purchase of inexpensive computers), and the vendor (who will promote models that have larger profit margins).

To ensure that the students learn the different tactics and how to use them effectively, you could employ the following sequence of breakout groups in an extended jigsaw activity:

---

40 My examples of tactics are adapted from those in Mnookin, R., Peppet, S., & Tulumello, A. (2004). *Beyond winning: Negotiating to create value in deals and disputes.* Cambridge, MA: Harvard University Press.

1. At the outset, you use a spreadsheet to set up breakout groups that each have four students. You specify an equal number of four different types of groups, each of which includes only one of the four stakeholders (e.g., separate groups for the faculty, separate groups for the tech staff, etc.). You ask students in each role to use two particular negotiating tactics in an upcoming negotiation; each role uses different tactics from the set you initially presented, which you have aligned to that role. For example, the students playing vendors might use anchoring and asking for a concession before providing a counter-offer, the students playing the tech staff might use belittling the alternative options and narrowly focusing on specific facts or considerations to push the negotiation their way, and so forth. You tell the students about the other roles—but you do not tell them which tactics the students playing the other roles will employ. Crucially, you tell the students that the next set of breakout groups will require them to negotiate with representatives of the other constituencies and you ask them to create a negotiation strategy that relies on their two assigned tactics (anticipating that other roles will be using the other tactics that were presented). These first groups meet for 10 minutes (and the students are aware of the total amount of time allocated).

2. When these groups end, you use another set of entries in the spreadsheet to reassign the students to new groups: Each of these second groups includes one member from each type of the initial groups (i.e., one representative from each of the four types of stakeholders).[41] You now tell the students that they are to role play a negotiation, with each representative using their assigned tactics to try to maximize their interests. In addition, you ask the students to infer the negotiation tactics being used by each of the other representatives—and tell them that they should evaluate how well those tactics are used and be prepared to justify their evaluations (note that the activity is designed to focus on the learning objectives of the lesson). These second groups meet for 5 minutes.

---

41 As of this writing, Zoom will only allow a user to create one set of breakout rooms with a spreadsheet in advance (this may change and may be different on other platforms). However, there are multiple other ways to assign students to sequences of breakout rooms. First, you can set up a spreadsheet in advance, indicating which room each student should go to for each group. You simply show the spreadsheet to the students immediately before each group, and ask them to look up their own assignment and to go to that room. If the class is relatively small (e.g., under 50 or so students), you can screen share the list within Zoom; if it is relatively large, you can either share the list in advance (e.g., emailing it or posting it on a bulletin board) or open it in another tab and ask students to search for their name. Second, you can pre-assign students for the first set of groups and then re-arrange students for the second phase by moving them manually into new groups, using spreadsheet entries as a guide. This works well enough with a couple of dozen students. Third, you can set up a second meeting in advance, and use a spreadsheet to set up new breakout groups for that meeting. In this case, at the end of the first set of breakouts the students would need to click on a new URL to join the new meeting, and then be reassigned to new groups. (Note: Other, less commonly used, platforms—such as the Foundry Forge—allow you to easily set up sequences of multiple breakout groups in advance and will automatically place students in the appropriate groups.)

3. When the second set of groups ends, you use the original spreadsheet entries to put the students back into their initial groups, the ones they were in at the very beginning of the activity. You ask each student to report to their group what they inferred to be the negotiation tactics used by each of the other stakeholders and their evaluation of each of those tactics. The four members of each group then discuss each member's observations and reach agreement on the best negotiation tactics that were employed by the other three stakeholders. These breakout groups end after 10 minutes.

4. Finally, the class as a whole reconvenes. If there are relatively few groups, you ask each one to report on their inferences about the negotiation tactics for one of the other stakeholders (selected at random, so the students could not focus only on one specific other stakeholder in the previous phase). The relevant groups provide feedback. If there are too many groups for all to report, you randomly can choose several groups to report. And you can end by asking the individual students to write down their inferences and evaluations, and grade those.

Figure 3.2 Negotiation Tactics Extended Jigsaw

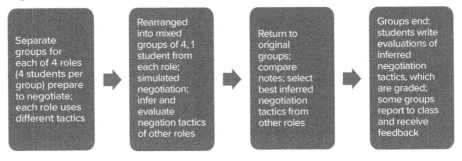

This sort of activity allows you to focus the students on the learning objectives. Moreover, it requires them to process the relevant information deeply, and hence be likely to learn it. And more than that, this exercise gives them experience in using the key information in ways that should transfer to the relevant situations at work or in daily life.

Finding the Goldilocks Spot

Students will learn when they use knowledge or skills in ways that induce the appropriate deep processing. But how should you decide how much mental processing to try to induce? It's clear that if you undershoot, the students will be bored; if you overshoot, they will be frustrated. You need to find the "Goldilocks spot," somewhere in the middle—where the amount of processing is not too little or too much, but just right.

This brings up a fundamental problem, which probably has bedeviled educators since classroom instruction began: Different students have different Goldilocks spots. What's "just right" for Noorjit may be too hard for Arthur, and what's just right for Arthur may be too hard for Juan.

One way to address this problem is to assign a tutor to each student. The tutor would be smart, well-informed, wise and sensitive, and would adjust instruction so that it was appropriate for the individual student. Were that we had a surplus supply of such people—and the finances to employ them! But alas, this solution does not scale.

Another way to try to deal with this problem is to program computers to mimic a gifted tutor. Many such programs now exist, falling under the general rubric of "Computer Aided Instruction," "Intelligent Computer Aided Instruction," "Adaptive Instruction," or "Personalized Learning."[42] Such programs can be useful, especially in domains where there is a clear correct answer. However, such systems have numerous problems.[43] For one, they are expensive to develop, sometimes requiring dozens—or even more—of hours of work for every hour of instruction.[44] For another, it sometimes is possible to "game" these systems, and get the right answers for the wrong reasons—and because there is no follow up, no one is the wiser. But more than this, students often simply don't want to interact with a machine; they want human, social interaction.

We can use technology in other ways to solve the "Goldilocks spot" problem at scale. One possible solution has two pieces (which my colleagues at Foundry College and I have used successfully in practice). The first is to compose breakout groups with students who have comparable relevant abilities. Quiz scores or polling results on similar material can be used for this purpose. Again, you can prepare a spreadsheet in advance, so that breakout groups include appropriate sets of students. In this case, having a column with the relevant assessment scores allows you to sort by such scores and then to assign consecutive clusters of the specified number of students to the same breakout groups.

---

42 Duchastel, P., & Imbeau, J. (1988). Intelligent computer-assisted instruction (ICAI): Flexible learning through better student-computer interaction. *Journal of Information Technology, 3*, 102-105; Mann, B.L. (2009). Computer-Aided Instruction. *Wiley Online Library*. 10.1002/9780470050118. ecse935; Singhal, A. (2018). The evolving state of AI-supplemented computer-assisted instruction. *EmergingEdTech*. https://www.emergingedtech.com/2018/05/artificial-intelligence-supplemented-computer-assisted-instruction/

43 Intelligent tutoring system. *Wikipedia*: https://en.wikipedia.org/wiki/Intelligent_tutoring_system

44 Hollands, F. M., & Devayani, T. (2014). Resource requirements and costs of developing and delivering MOOCs. *The International Review of Research in Open and Distributed Learning, 15*, no. 5; Murray, T. (1999). Authoring intelligent tutoring systems: An analysis of the state of the art. *International Journal of Artificial Intelligence in Education, 10*, 98–129.

The second piece—used in conjunction with the first—is to construct the activity itself so that it can be approached at multiple levels, so that students can drill more or less deeply into it. For example, if you are teaching students about ambiguity, you might put them in breakout groups and ask them to read a series of paragraphs and identify everything that is ambiguous. Some of the ambiguity is very blatant, such as clearly ambiguous words that are easily identified by everyone; but some of the ambiguity is more subtle (e.g., emerging from relations across different sentences). Depending on how good the groups are at this sort of analysis, they will uncover different numbers of the more subtle examples.

The central idea is that the members of each group nudge each other to the Goldilocks spot for that group (they were assigned so that the members of the group are likely to have very similar Goldilocks spots), and approach the task in a way that is neither boring nor frustrating for them.

What about the idea that groups with mixed levels of ability are good for everyone because the stronger students learn by teaching and the weaker ones benefit from their help? I've sometimes heard an analogy to tennis: It's best to play with someone better than you are; that's how you'll learn best. Maybe so, but only if the stronger player is willing to teach, and knows how to do so—and the weaker player doesn't mind having a peer play this role. Previous experience has convinced me that these assumptions are not always warranted.

Taking a step back, the goal is to create situations that induce deep processing (and hence promote learning, which is what this is all about). We don't want to bore or frustrate students, by making the activity too easy or too hard. A better tennis analogy is to exercise: Two beginners playing each other can get just as much exercise as two champions playing each other. And exercise is the analogy to mental processing: people at a lower level can be induced to do just as much mental processing as people at a higher level, and hence both will learn.[45]

To be clear, I'm not suggesting that breakout groups always be composed of students at the same level of the relevant knowledge or ability. If material is difficult to understand, it makes sense to have a range of students in each breakout group and ensure that at least some of them understand it well enough

45 The results of studies of heterogeneous versus homogeneous groups are mixed, and I have done my best to distill the bottom line here. See, for example: Marzano, R. J., Pickering, D., & Pollock, J. E. (2001). *Classroom instruction that works: Research-based strategies for increasing student achievement.* Alexandria, VA: Association for Supervision and Curriculum Development; Kulik, C. C., & Kulik, J. A.. (1982). Effects of ability grouping on secondary school students: A meta-analysis of evaluation findings. *American Educational Research Journal, 19,* https://doi.org/10.3102/00028312019003415; Lou, Y., Abrami, P. C., Poulsen, C., Chambers, B., & d'Apollonia, S. (1996). Within-class grouping: A meta-analysis. *Review of Educational Research, 66,* 423-458; Schullery, N. M., & Schullery, S. E. (2006). Are heterogeneous or homogeneous groups more beneficial to students? *Journal of Management Education, 30,* 542-556.

to know how to do the activity (we don't want the blind leading the blind). But if the to-be-learned knowledge or skills are relatively straightforward, the objective often may be to help the students cement the information in memory and help them learn how to apply the information across a wide range of situations. In these cases, it makes sense to group students at the same level and to use multilayered assignments to allow each group to nudge themselves to their Goldilocks spot.

In short, an activity can be structured so that students will engage in the relevant deep processing, which helps them achieve a specific learning outcome. You need to design the activity so that the right kind of processing occurs to achieve this end. The beauty of this approach is that the students learn as a byproduct of engaging in the mental processing, even if they are not particularly interested in learning that material. In the following chapters, we see many additional ways to induce and buttress deep processing.

—4—

Chunking

Every instructor knows that it's a bad idea to present too much material in a lecture. But how much is too much? Researchers have found that we humans can take in only about three or four "chunks" at a time.[46] To get a sense for what a "chunk" is, glance at the following letters for a few seconds and try to memorize them in order:

XXCBSCIAIBMNBCXX

Now look away from the letters and try to recall them. How many of the letters could you memorize after a glance?

Now try it again, but use this hint: Look for three-letter acronyms of famous organizations. How many can you recall now?

Most people can memorize the entire string when they look for these acronyms. I could have achieved the same goal by printing CBS in green, CIA in red, IBM in blue, and NBC in yellow. Or I could have achieved the same result simply by inserting a space between the groups of three letters, as in: CBS CIA IBM NBC. In both of these cases, by adding colors or spaces, I help you to organize the individual letters into units, which are called chunks.

It's almost impossible to memorize 16 separate letters at a glance, but it's not so hard if you organize the letters into chunks. And this effect is not just about letters, or even just visual material; any information can be organized into chunks.

---

46 Cowan, N. (2001). The magical number 4 in short-term memory: A reconsideration of mental storage capacity. *Behavioral and Brain Sciences, 24*, 87–114.

The Principle of Chunking states that "Learning is easier when material is organized into three or four organized units, each of which itself can contain three or four units."

A particularly impressive example of chunking was reported in 1980 by a team of researchers at Carnegie Mellon University in Pittsburg.[47] They studied a single student over the course of about a year and a half. This volunteer came into the lab to be tested at least three times per week. The study was deceptively simple: Each second, the researchers simply read aloud a digit from a list of random digits, and the participant repeated back the list after it had been read. The researchers began with a list that was only one digit long. They read the digit, and the participant repeated it back. The researchers then read a list with two randomly selected digits, and the participant repeated them back. The researchers increased the size of the list of new random digits until the participant could no longer repeat them back accurately. That first day, he correctly recalled seven digits, which is average. The next session picked up where the previous one had ended. Every list was different, consisting of a new series of randomly selected digits. The length of the lists grew steadily longer over time as the participant improved. When the researchers finally called it quits, the participant could repeat back a new list of 79 random digits.

At the end of the very first session, the participant faltered after seven digits— what changed over time that allowed him eventually to recall 79 digits? The trick was that the participant developed clever ways to organize digits into chunks, and—crucially—to organize each of these individual chunks so that they in turn were grouped into larger chunks (each of which was composed of three or four smaller chunks). Specifically, this participant had run in numerous marathon races, and could recall the time he took for various segments of these races or he could recall times of races he ran early or late in his career. He was able to convert a set of random digits into specific times for a segment of a race. For example, if the string of digits was "3, 4, 9, 2," he could relate these numbers to the time he recalled: "3 minutes and 49 point 2 seconds, near world-record mile time." (p. 1181). This strategy allowed him to replace what were four separate entities with a single chunk. He could then organize sets of these segments into a larger group, creating an even larger chunk. As he worked out such strategies, he broadened his approach and came to organize some of the digits into specific people's ages or highly memorable dates.[48]

---

47 Ericsson, K. A., Chase, W. G., & Faloon, S. (1980). Acquisition of a memory skill. *Science, 208*, 1181-1182.

48 This finding has been replicated and extended; see, for example, Yoon, J-S., Ericsson, K. A., & Donatelli, D. (2018). Effects of 30 years of disuse on exceptional memory performance. *Cognitive Science, 42*, 884-903.

The results of this study illustrate two key facts about how our minds work when we are learning: The first is that we store information as organized units, not individual isolated bits; the second is that each of these units in turn can be part of a larger unit. The combination of these two factors allows us to process and take in an enormous amount of information.

Many teachers use chunking to organize their courses into sections, modules or units, and the Principle of Chunking speaks directly to how lessons should be organized. One way to think about this is in terms of learning objectives. You can specify an overarching learning objective for a lesson, such as "Master key techniques used in negotiation." Then you can have more specific learning objectives, each of which may focus on a particular technique, such as using methods of persuasion or setting up in advance a backup plan in case negotiations fail. And these learning objectives themselves in turn can have smaller chunks, such as characteristics of a good backup plan (e.g., it is likely to be appealing to key stakeholders, is not very expensive, and can be implemented easily).

You can also use this principle to design activities within lessons. For example, let's say that you were teaching Five Paragraph Form, which is a simple format that students can use to write an essay. The first paragraph identifies three aspects or examples that bear on the topic, then each of them is addressed in a separate paragraph, and then there's a concluding paragraph that pulls it all together. (Note that this parses into three big chunks: the introductory paragraph, the set of three explanatory paragraphs, and the concluding paragraph—and that middle chunk itself contains three sub-chunks, one for each of the points introduced initially.) To teach this format, you could give students in breakout groups a brief (even just a single page long) run-on document (with no paragraph demarcations) and ask them to parse it, to identify where the boundaries are between the first paragraph and the discussion of the first example, between that and the discussion of the second example, and so on. This chunking activity not only will teach them about the value of organizing into units, but it also will induce deep processing that focuses on the content matter.

Let's say that you were teaching about story structure more generally. You could do the same thing with stories, but now the paragraph boundaries are not so clear—and hence after breakout groups end it would be interesting to learn how students justify their decisions about where the paragraph boundaries should be. Again, this activity induces deep processing of relevant information.

And if your primary learning objective is that students should understand the conceptual structure of a domain, you could use this same approach by asking students where to insert headings in a document that discusses that material. To drill down on this, you can ask the students to insert both "A-level headings" for major sections and "B-level headings" for sections within those sections.

In all cases, materials used in activities should be designed to be as simple as possible (but, to paraphrase Albert Einstein, no simpler than that). Students should not be required to take in more than three or four overarching chunks when reading instructions, when using a diagram, and so on—and each of these overarching chunks should contain no more than three or four sub-chunks.[49]

Using Chunking to Organize Lessons

Many instructors already recognize the value of active learning, but relatively few know how to implement it well—and I suspect that many are nervous about transitioning their courses to an online setting (either synchronous, via a platform such as Google Meet, Webex or Zoom, or asynchronous via text, video recordings or PowerPoint decks administered through Canvas, Blackboard, or some other Learning Management System). However, upgrading need not be onerous or intimidating, and now is the perfect time to take an existing lesson plan that doesn't involve active learning and upgrade it to make learning more effective and stimulating for students and, in turn, make your experience more rewarding as an instructor.

In order to upgrade a course, the course designer (who typically is the instructor) needs to answer three questions: How can active learning exercises be squeezed into the lecture, given time constraints? Where should active learning exercises be inserted in a lesson plan? And, what should be included in active learning exercises?

Here's a simple way to use the Principle of Chunking to answer these questions. This approach works equally well for front-loaded and back-loaded Learning Sandwiches.

1. Identify core material. You should use active learning exercises to address core material, and thus the first step is to identify the core material in each lesson. One way to do this is to go to the assessments you use to grade students in the course. For simplicity, let's say that you use three tests: two midterms and a final exam. Look at each question on your exams and go back to your lectures and circle the section where the answer to that question was provided. (If the question was answered only in readings, consider whether that material should be included in the lecture—if it's important enough to test, perhaps it's important enough to emphasize in a lesson.) If you don't have a transcript of your lectures to use to identify core material, you can either transcribe them or record yourself giving the lecture, and have the recording converted to text.

---

49 cf. Chandler, P., & Sweller, J. (1991). Cognitive load theory and the format of instruction. *Cognition and Instruction, 8*, 293-332.

(This can be done quickly and easily via a service such as Amazon's automated Transcribe program or a free service such as NCH Software.)

This process, if followed literally, would require a lot of time. However, if you wrote both the lectures and exams, you can do this exercise informally: Just go through your lecture notes and identify the sections where you want to test the students.

The areas you identified in your lectures are clearly what you think are most important, which is why you assess the students' knowledge of these pieces in your exams. Everything in your lectures should directly address the learning objectives you had in mind for each lesson, which is what the exam questions should have assessed.

To answer that first question, how to squeeze in active learning exercises: Focus on the core material and try to eliminate as much as possible of everything else. If you do this, you should have plenty of room for active learning exercises.

2. Next, chunk your lesson by core material. Consult the portions of your lecture that were important enough to test, and see whether you can group them to create mini-lectures (for front loaded Learning Sandwiches) or instances where you frame a problem or issue to introduce a learning objective (for back-loaded Learning Sandwiches). Are four or fewer contiguous parts of the original lecture tightly related, forming a larger chunk? If so, then put a breakout group or other type of activity right after that chunk.

If the identified areas don't line up to form larger chunks or you have more than three or four of the larger chunks, consider whether you are trying to cram too much into one lecture. The students will have difficulty organizing and taking in so many distinct pieces of knowledge or components of skills. There's really little point in trying to cover a large amount of material if the students aren't going to be able to learn it.

If you have a series of small chunks that don't cluster into larger ones but do tightly cohere as a narrative, the entire lecture may function as a single chunk. Now you need to decide which of these small chunks needs to be emphasized. You will be faced with the same issue if you have more than three or four larger chunks, or if you simply don't have time for more than one or two breakout groups or other active learning exercises.

To answer that second question, where to insert active learning exercises: After a larger chunk or after a smaller one that needs to be emphasized.

3. Finally, after you identify where to insert active learning, you need to decide what to focus on in the active learning exercise itself—what to have them

mentally process deeply. Consider the core material that immediately precedes an active learning exercise and decide what are the hardest aspects to understand, remember, or apply. Active learning is a way to help students master difficult material, so you can use it selectively to address just such material. Use activities (such as those summarized in Chapter 10) that draw on the learning principles to help the students master the most challenging aspects of the learning objective.

Figure 4.1 Chunking a Lecture

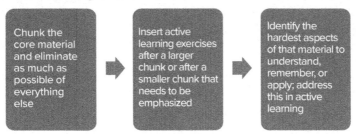

This approach is not limited to synchronous teaching, where you teach live classes via Google Meet, Webex, Zoom or the like. You can use the Principle of Chunking in exactly the same way if you pre-record lectures, where students would pause after you've presented a major chunk and then do something— even if that "something" is only to write a paraphrase of what they've heard, which then is evaluated by a teaching assistant or another student. In later chapters I will have many suggestions about how to use active learning in asynchronous settings (and Chapter 10 offers many possible types of exercises).

Speaking of pausing: It's sometimes not clear to non-experts exactly where the boundaries are between chunks. Thus, when delivering a lecture, pausing or being explicit about transitions between chunks can be very helpful for students.

The Principle of Chunking is all about organizing material so that humans can easily absorb it. Given your goal of helping such humans to learn, this principle can be invaluable. Moreover, this principle is especially useful when combined with the Principle of Deep Processing: Appropriate chunking directs students to process deeply what they need to know. And, more than that, such mental processing leads students to store essential information in memory in ways that help them later to use this information—as we see in the following chapter.

—5—

Building
Associations

The Principle of Associations states that "Learning is enhanced by associating new information to what is already known." Here's a nice demonstration of how using associations can help students learn.[50] Researchers read students the passage below and then asked them to recall it. The trick of the study was that half of the students were read the passage cold, with no title, whereas the other half first were given a title that could help them associate the material together. Here is the passage:

❝ The procedure is actually quite simple. First you arrange things into different groups... Of course, one pile may be sufficient depending on how much there is to do. If you have to go somewhere else due to lack of facilities that is the next step, otherwise you are pretty well set. It is important not to overdo any particular endeavor. That is, it is better to do too few things at once than too many. In the short run this may not seem important, but complications from doing too many can easily arise. A mistake can be expensive as well... At first the whole procedure will seem complicated. Soon, however, it will become just another facet of life. It is difficult to foresee any end to the necessity for this task in the immediate future, but then one never can tell. After the procedure is completed one arranges the materials into different groups again. Then they can be put into their appropriate places. Eventually

---

50 Bransford, J., & Johnson, M. (1972). Contextual prerequisites for understanding: Some investigations of comprehension and recall. *Journal of Verbal Learning & Verbal Behavior, 11,* 717–726. The passage is on p. 722.

they will be used once more and the whole cycle will have to be repeated. However, that is part of life. **"**

Most of the students in the group that did not receive the title had trouble even understanding the passage, and did terribly when later asked to recall it. In contrast, the students in the group that received the title "Washing Clothes" did well. Why? The title provided a key to how to associate the individual items, both to each other and to the broader central theme.

We already saw an example of the power of associations in the previous chapter, when I described the remarkable case of a student who was able to memorize 79 random digits, hearing each digit read aloud one second after the previous one. In that chapter I emphasized the fact that he had constructed chunks, based largely on his knowledge of times he required to run races. I noted but didn't emphasize the fact that he was using prior associations to create these chunks. And the same is true for the chunks you created at the outset of that chapter, where you associated letters into familiar acronyms (such as IBM and CBS). But the power of using associations during learning extends far beyond their role in chunking.

Making and using associations is important not just because you can use them to organize material when you are first taking it in; associations also can help you integrate what you are learning into what you already know, which makes the information "stick" in your memory. This fact helps to explain what some researchers thought of as a paradox: The more you know about a topic, the easier it is to learn even more about it.[51] This fact can seem paradoxical if you think of long-term memory like a very large filing cabinet—which leads to the intuition that the more it is filled, the less space there is for something new. However, it's better to think of memory like a giant hat rack where the more hats you have, the more branches and hooks you add—and hence the more places you then have to hang even more hats.

In addition to helping you organize information and store it in memory, associations can help you to dig information out of memory when you want to recall it. For example, have you ever had difficulty remembering the names of people you meet? If so, here's a simple technique that can help: When you meet someone, say someone named Sam, and want to learn their name, immediately think of another person you already know who has the same name. Then look for facial features of the new person that remind you of your previous acquaintance.

---

51 Reder, L. M., & Anderson, J. R. (1980). A partial resolution of the paradox of interference: The role of integrating knowledge. *Cognitive Psychology, 12,* 447–472; Smith, E. E., Adams, N., & Schorr, D. (1978). Fact retrieval and the paradox of interference. *Cognitive Psychology, 10,* 438–464.

For example, they might have similar eyebrows or their cheek bones might be similar. Then associate this feature or features with the previous person and their name. When you later see the new person, just look at their face until you hit on the feature or features that remind you of that previous acquaintance, which then will allow you to recall their name. The associations you create when you first learn the person's name thus can help you later to recall it.

In this example, you would have engaged in active learning: You first actively recalled someone else with the same name, searched for shared features that later will remind you of the connection, and then stored the associations in memory. The Principle of Deep Processing again applies here, but now in the context of cementing new associations that you have set up.

Designing Lessons

The Principle of Associations has clear implications for how to design lessons. For a start, begin with foundational material and build up from there. This idea is clearly illustrated with the Washing Clothes study: Once you know the title of the passage, everything else falls into place.

The idea of starting with the foundational material fits neatly into the idea of defining your learning objectives at several levels of granularity. To begin, you need to identify the overarching learning objective or objectives for a lesson, which should serve to link everything you discuss. Then consider more specific learning outcomes that you want the students to achieve and how they are related. For example, your overarching learning objective might be "Identify what we can learn from the Covid-19 Pandemic that could help us in the next pandemic." The specific learning outcomes might include the students knowing the facts about how the virus is transmitted (e.g., via droplets and contact), ways to minimize transmission (social distancing, masks, hand washing), effects on the economy, on international trade, and on immigration. You should be explicit about the connections among these factors, both the direct connections (e.g., how disruption of international trade disrupted the economy) and indirect ones (e.g., how disruption of international trade affected attitudes about immigration via the tightening economy). As the course designer, you should put yourself in the students' shoes and take their perspective, thinking about how they can associate the different parts of the lesson. You want the students to be like the group that got the "Washing Clothes" label, not the group that was left to organize the material on its own.

The Principle of Associations leads you to design active learning exercises with the same reasoning: Start with the material that is closest to the overarching learning objective, the central facts and concepts that will help the students to tie together (i.e., associate) much of what follows. You might want to devote an activity to the foundational concepts at the outset, before you get into details. If students have a shaky foundation, it's going to be difficult to build on top of it. Where you start (i.e., what the initial foundation is) depends on what the students already know, and early in the term it's worth conducting a survey to get some sense of their background knowledge.

Spaced Practice and Varied Context

One way to lead students to learn useful associations is to use spaced practice. Anyone who has painted a wall quickly learns the truth of the old adage that "two thin coats are better than one thick coat." The same is true for learning: Students learn more effectively if they are asked to use previously taught information repeatedly during a course.[52]

Spaced practice is effective in part because it allows students to associate different contexts to the same material, which later provides more possible cues to help them recall that material. Here's a vivid demonstration of the role of cues in recall:[53] Researchers asked participants to learn words either while sitting on the shore or while in scuba gear, 20 feet under water; they later tested the participants' memory for the words either while they were sitting on the shore or were under water. The researchers tested every combination of learning situation and testing situation: Participants learned on land and were tested on land; learned on land and were tested under water; learned under water and were tested on land; and learned under water and were tested under water. The results were dramatic: The participants recalled about 50% more words when they learned and recalled the words in the same situation (either both on land or both under water). Switching contexts between learning and testing resulted in much poorer recall.

What's going on here? When we dig something out of memory, we use cues to help us locate that information (this is the key to the method for learning names of new acquaintances I described earlier). When you learn something, you associate it with the context where you learned it. The context includes not just the physical surroundings (such as being on land or under water), but also factors such as your physical and emotional state, what you were thinking about recently, and your desires and expectations. And because you associated these

52 Custers, E.J. (2010). Long term retention of basic science knowledge: A review study. *Advances in Health Science Education, 15,* 109–128; Kooloos, J. G. M., Bergman, E. M., Scheffers, M. A. G. P., Schepens-Franke, A. N., & Vostenbosch, A. T. M. (2019). The effect of passive and active education methods applied in repetition activities on the retention of anatomical knowledge. *Anatomical Sciences Education, 13,* 458-466.

53 Godden, D. R., & Baddeley, A. D. (1975). Context-dependent memory in two natural environments: On land and underwater. *British Journal of Psychology, 66,* 325-331.

factors with what you are learning, it's easier later to dig the information out of memory when you are in the presence of the associated information (which serves as cues to prompt your memory).

The land/under water study demonstrates what happens when only one context has been associated with learned material. The goal of spaced practice is to avoid the situation illustrated by this study—to be able to recall information in many different situations, not just the single one where you learned the information.

A simple way to have the students engage in spaced practice is to include a quick quiz at the end of every class, which includes five or six questions—and have one or two of them randomly drawn from a prior lesson, addressing a learning objective that was covered before. Requiring students to recall earlier material repeatedly over time will lead them to form new associations that later can be used during recall.

You can boost the benefits of spaced practice by intentionally having students learn in very different contexts. Doing so creates more associations that later can be used to dig information out of storage. One way to create multiple contexts is simple: I lave students participate in different active learning exercises that cover the same material; these exercises need not be very long, but they should be clearly different (Chapter 10 offers many choices). You can also revisit earlier material in combination with new material. This is particularly easy to do in STEM (Science, Technology, Engineering, Mathematics) fields, where new material clearly builds on earlier material.

Another way to provide contextual cues is to induce emotion, which can easily be associated with information to aid later recall.[54] Here's an example of how to do that, which employs a winnowing procedure to boil down the responses to few enough cases to discuss all of them during the debrief after breakout groups end:

1. You ask students to formulate a situation in which the to-be-learned material produces a positive emotion, such as happiness; you then have them repeat the exercise, but now ask them to produce a negative emotion, such as guilt.

2. To motivate students, you then pair each group with another group and ask them to select the best example that used a positive emotion and the best example that used a negative emotion. This is easy to do online.

---

54 McGaugh, J.L. (2003). *Memory and emotion: The making of lasting memories.* New York: Columbia University Press

3. You then pair one of these larger groups with another large group and do the same thing. This process winnows down the number of examples. After breakout groups end, the remaining examples are then presented to the class as a whole, which votes on the best ones.

4. Finally, to ensure that students were in fact engaged, you ask each student to write reasons why the winning examples were in fact the best—or to write a "dissenting opinion" that indicates why the student disagreed with the vote. These evaluations are then graded.

However, I recommend that only mild emotions be used in this way. Although the literature is mixed, there is evidence that strong negative emotions can actually interfere with learning.[55]

Figure 5.1 Winnowing Procedure

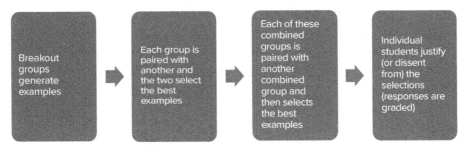

Organizing Examples

The Principle of Associations bears on how students should organize information they take in, how they should integrate new information into what they already know, and how they should associate retrieval cues to help them later access the information. As part of all of these functions, an important role of the Principle of Associations is to help students understand the material. In particular, you can take abstract material and make it much more comprehensible and memorable by providing examples. But the examples by themselves aren't enough; you need to tie them together by indicating what they have in common. This situation is a bit like the "Washing Clothes" example discussed earlier: Without the principle, the examples may seem disconnected and unrelated.

---

55 For example, see Lang, A. Newhangen, J., & Reeves, B. (1996). Negative video as structure: Emotion, attention, capacity, and memory. *Journal of Broadcasting and Electronic Media, 40*, 460-477 (as cited in Schwartz, D. L., Tsang, J. M., & Blair, K. P. (2016). *The ABCs of how we learn: 26 scientifically proven approaches, how they work, and when to use them*. New York: W.W. Norton, p. 311.)

You can flip this exercise on its ear. Instead of providing the principle that ties together a set of examples or other material (e.g., observations, facts, concepts), you can present disconnected examples or other material and ask the students to arrange them into a coherent whole—and then to explain the rationale for their organization. Again, an added benefit of such active learning is that students will engage in deep processing of the relevant information—which will enhance their learning the associations.

You can use active learning in many ways to help students build appropriate associations. For example, you can help students create and use associations by asking them to generate stories. For instance, say that you want students to learn about the economies of the United States versus Germany just prior to World War I. You could ask groups of several students to produce a story about two companies (one in each country) that were engaged in a trade deal. The students are told to create the story to illustrate key differences in how the economies worked. You could then have pairs of groups evaluate each other's stories, using a rubric that focuses on how well the stories associated the key characteristics with the two countries.

The key to drawing on this learning principle is to decide in advance what learning outcomes you want the students to achieve and then to decide which associations will help the students organize the material, store it effectively in memory, and then have sufficient associated cues to be able to retrieve it later.

—6—

Dual Coding

Is a picture really worth 1,000 words? The answer probably depends on the particular picture and words. In any case, learning—and subsequent memory—will be greatly enhanced not just by showing a picture but by combining pictures and words. This is true for several reasons, but an intriguing one is that different parts of the brain process visual information and language—and areas of the brain that process input often also store that information in memory. When students learn based on both pictures and words, their brains have two shots at storing the information, one visual and one verbal.

The Principle of Dual Coding states that "Learning is more effective when material is presented as both words and images."[56] Dual Coding gains its force from using two "codes," words and images; images can be visual, auditory, or in any modality. Lectures can be more effective by combining words with illustrations, videos, and demonstrations. But more than that, active learning exercises can be especially effective when they lead students to create or use both types of codes.

Perhaps the simplest way to exploit this principle during active learning is to ask students to illustrate the to-be-learned knowledge or skills: You can ask students to search the internet to find appropriate pictures to illustrate what you've taught, which may involve arranging the pictures appropriately (especially if you've taught them about an event that unfolds over time).

---

56 Kosslyn, S. M. (1994). *Image and brain*. Cambridge, MA: MIT Press; Mayer, R. E. (2001). *Multimedia learning*. NY: Cambridge University Press; Paivio, A. (1971). *Imagery and verbal processes*. New York: Holt, Rinehart, and Winston; Mayer, R. E., & Moreno, R. (2003). Nine ways to reduce cognitive load in multimedia learning. *Educational Psychologist, 38*, 43-52.

This exercise will maximize key findings about dual coding: The combined power of words and images is strongest if the two are close to each other, both in time and space.[57] Moreover, the mere effort of searching to find an appropriate image is itself a learning aid: Not only will the students remember the words and images themselves, but also the effort of searching for and evaluating candidate images will engage deep processing—which also aids learning.

As usual when designing active learning exercises, it's good to have students interacting, which motivates them to pay attention and to do well (if only because they rarely want to let down their peers or look bad in front of them). It's easy to use online platforms (e.g., Google Meet, Webex, or Zoom) to create pairs of students and ask them to search for appropriate images. Following this, you could join each pair with another pair and ask them to evaluate the images the other pair produced (and vice versa). These evaluations should focus on how well the images illustrate the desired knowledge or skills. Moreover, these evaluations could serve as a prompt for students to find better illustrations; the two pairs need not be in competition—they can help each other. As mentioned earlier, when you grade the final results, this need not be a zero-sum game; various "cooperative learning" techniques can ensure that all boats rise with a rising tide. For example, you can give students a bonus if both pairs that are grouped together score over a certain amount, which will motivate them to help each other learn.[58]

Illustrating Concepts

The Principle of Dual Coding implies more than that you should ask students to find or create illustrations of specific knowledge or skills. The principle is much broader than that. For example, one way to invoke this principle is to use it in combination with the Principle of Associations by asking students to use Mind Mapping to organize a set of knowledge or skills.[59] A Mind Map is a visual way to lay out ideas and indicate how they are related to each other. You can think of a Mind Map by analogy to a hub-and-spokes subway system, where there is a central station (which represents the core knowledge or skills) that is connected to smaller stations (which represent related knowledge or skills) and then individual branches that extend to particular destinations (which represent specific knowledge or skills). You can use colors to code the different types of

---

57 Mayer, R. (2009). *Multimedia learning (2nd edition)*. Cambridge: Cambridge University Press.

58 Slavin, R. E. (2014). Making cooperative learning powerful. *Educational Leadership, 72*, 22-26.

59 Farrand, P., Hussain, F., & Hennessy, E. (2002). The efficacy of the mind map study technique. *Medical Education, 36*, 426–431; Nesbit, J.C., & Adesope, O.O. (2006). Learning with concept and knowledge maps: A meta-analysis. *Review of Educational Research, 76*, 413–448.

material and also include names and symbols. You can also label the tracks that connect the stations, to indicate how knowledge or skills are related.[60]

Here is an example of a Mind Map[61] used to illustrate the concept of a Mind Map!

Figure 6.1 A Mind Map

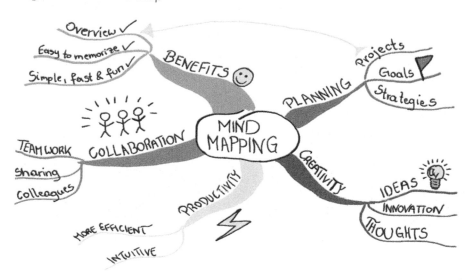

Let's consider how you could use a Mind Map to teach the five principles presented in this book. You could place the students into breakout groups and ask them to create a Mind Map that illustrates each principle, its characteristics, and its best applications.

1. The students first discuss what should be at the hub, what is the central piece of knowledge or component of a skill. In this case, the core idea is the science of learning.

2. The students then discuss what the main branches should be, which radiate out from the central hub. They should have a branch for each of the five principles.

3. After identifying the main branches, students should identify secondary and tertiary branches (e.g., for each of the principles, they indicate key characteristics, contexts in which is it particularly useful, and perhaps direct links to other principles that it works particularly well with).

---

60 See, for example, Mind Map, https://en.wikipedia.org/wiki/Mind_map; https://www.mindmapping.com

61 Image by Raphaela Brandner, www.mindmeister.com, reprinted with permission; see https://www.mindmeister.com/blog/why-mind-mapping/

4. The students create the diagram, with branches for each associated idea or characteristic and branches that connect them. The students not only should think of memorable images to represent each idea (e.g., the central idea of the science of learning might be represented by an image of a brain) but also—in keeping with the Principle of Dual Coding—think of simple ways to label each. (It's the combination of words and images that is so powerful.) The images could be photos the students take, drawings they create, or images they find on the internet. And again, such an activity also invokes deep processing, which boosts learning. (You might now be thinking that you would like to see such a Mind Map of this book, and—in the spirit of active learning—I encourage you to create one!)

Figure 6.2 Creating a Mind Map

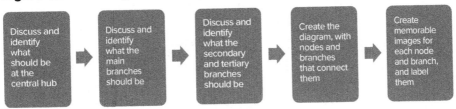

Notice that my use of flowcharts in this book illustrates the Principle of Dual Coding: Not only do the flowcharts complement the text, but also the charts themselves combine graphic elements (the boxes and arrows) with text. I aim to show and tell.

Numerous web applications are available to help students create Mind Maps.[62] If breakout groups are in a web-based video conferencing platform, one student can open a Mind Map app in another tab and screen share with the other students in the group—and the group as a whole can work on creating the chart. Alternatively, the students can use a shared whiteboard or drawing tool to collaborate on producing the illustration.

Using Charts, Graphs and Diagrams

Mind Maps are a special type of chart. In general, charts organize qualitative information, making clear what the relations are among the elements; to do

62 Santos, D. (15 February 2013). Top 10 totally free mind mapping software tools. IMDevin: https://web.archive.org/web/20130807152823/http://www.imdevin.com/top-10-totally-free-mind-mapping-software-tools/; for paid tools, some of which offer a large range of options, see https://mashable.com/2013/09/25/mind-mapping-tools/ .

so, charts use lines or arrows to connect boxes, shapes, pictures of objects, or even just words. You can ask students to create charts when they are learning about the structure of an object, organization or event. Numerous apps allow students to create charts, which can be accessed in another tab during online learning. Depending on what you are teaching, you can use different types of charts in active learning exercises, which will lead students to use both pictures and words when learning.

Charts are particularly useful for illustrating how a sequence of events unfolds over time. For instance, the familiar flowchart can be used to lay out a physical process, a set of social interactions, or any events that have discrete phases (such as a series of breakout groups!). Asking students to create such a chart will not only lead them to think clearly about the relationships among the entities but also to recall both the verbal descriptions and the illustration.

Other sorts of charts show how entities are organized hierarchically. For example, if the instructor is teaching about the structure of an organization, a hierarchical "tree" chart can nicely illustrate who reports to whom. Such a chart is even more memorable if at each level students are asked to find illustrations (e.g., on the internet) of the entity. For example, if you were teaching about the structure of the Federal Government, you could ask the students to locate pictures of key buildings or individuals (current or historical) for each level.

The Principle of Dual Coding can also be drawn upon by asking students to produce a diagram, which is an abstracted picture of an object or event. Diagrams typically show just the most important aspects of the object, leaving out the sorts of details about the surface, color and texture you would find in a photograph. Although the parts of diagrams are literal depictions of parts of the corresponding object, diagrams use a combination of symbols (such as arrows), pictures and words to structure information. If you've ever assembled furniture from Ikea, put together an exercise bike, or built a model airplane from a kit, you've had a diagram to help you assemble it. The diagram may not have been as useful as it could have been because it either failed to show the parts clearly (perhaps because they were too small) or failed to show how they fit together clearly (perhaps because the arrows did not connect parts precisely).

If you are teaching quantitative relationships, you can also draw on the Principle of Dual Coding by having students construct or evaluate graphs. Again, numerous apps are available to make this easy to do online. Whereas charts and diagrams illustrate qualitative relations among entities, graphs illustrate quantitative relations—the relations among measured amounts. In all cases, graphs obey the "More is More" rule: The higher the bar, higher the line, or larger the wedge in a pie, the more of some quantity is being shown.[63]

Figure 6.3 A Simple Graph Shown to Undergraduates

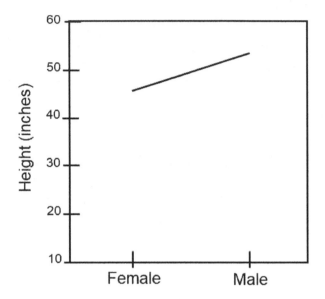

Graphs are surprisingly hard for many students to understand and produce. My favorite example, which is by no means an isolated or exceptional case, is a study in which researchers showed Stanford University students a simple line graph like the one in Figure 6.3 above. This graph compares the heights of males and females. When the students were asked to interpret what they saw, 12% of them claimed that "The more male a person is, the taller he/she is."[64] Some people find this sort of result difficult to believe, and try to explain it in terms of "bad graphs" or the like. For example, in this case one could argue that line graphs should only be used when there are continuous variations along the X axis, and thus the students' assumption of continuous variation makes sense; however, others argue that such graphs should also be used to show differences by providing a slope (which thereby relieves the viewer of the effort of imagining a line that connects two bars or the like). In any case, such graphs are in fact used,

63 Kosslyn, S. M. (2006). *Graph design for the eye and mind*. New York. Oxford University Press.

64 Zacks, J., & Tversky, B. (1999). Bars and lines: A study of graphic communication. *Memory & Cognition, 27*, 1073–1079.

and students should know how to read them—but they often do not.[65] Thus, you cannot take for granted that students will in fact understand charts and graphs. Rather, taking advantage of the Principle of Dual Coding in conjunction with the Principle of Deep Processing, you can ask students to describe what is being shown—and correct this if necessary. In so doing, students gain the benefits of processing both visual and verbal information.

Visualizing Illustrations

Finally, the Principle of Dual Coding can be used even without showing the students a picture: Students can be asked to "supply their own picture" by visualizing, by creating a mental picture in their "mind's eye." Recall my favorite experiment in cognitive psychology, which I summarized in Chapter 3: The researcher presented a series of pairs of words and asked the participants either to silently verbalize the words or to visualize the named objects interacting in some way (e.g., for the pair "cow-tree" they might visualize a cow rubbing against a tree). When the participants' memories were tested later, the researcher found that visualizing objects results in about twice as many word pairs later being recalled than were recalled after verbalizing them. In Chapter 3, I emphasized that this finding reflects how much deep mental processing was required to do the two tasks. In Chapter 3 we also saw that what students remember depends on which information is processed deeply (for example about sounds versus meaning). What I didn't mention previously is that students can be led to process deeply more than one type of information about the material, which enhances learning even more. To create mental images in that experiment, the participants needed to process both the names (to understand them and dig out the corresponding visual memory) and the previously stored visual information itself. In so doing, they were creating two kinds of new memories of the pair: One verbal (the names themselves) and one visual (how the named objects

---

65 Delmas, R., Garfield, J., & Ooms, A. (2005). Using assessment items to study students' difficulty reading and interpreting graphical representations of distributions. In K. Makar (Ed.), *Proceedings of the Fourth International Research Forum on Statistical Reasoning, Literacy, and Reasoning*. Auckland, NZ: University of Auckland; Friel, S. N., Curcio, F., & Bright, G. W. (2001). Making sense of graphs: Critical factors influencing comprehension and instructional implications. *Journal for Research in Mathematics Education, 32*, 124-158; Glazer, N. (2011). Challenges with graph interpretation: a review of the literature. *Studies in Science Education, 47,* 183-210; Shah, P. (2002). Graph comprehension: The role of format, content, and individual difference. In M. Anderson, B. Mayer & P. Olivier (Eds.), *Diagrammatic representation and reasoning* (pp. 207–222). London & New York: Springer Verlag; Shah, P., & Carpenter, P.A. (1995). Conceptual limitations in comprehending line graphs. *Journal of Experimental Psychology, 124*, 43–61; Shah, P., & Hoeffner, J. (2002). Review of graph comprehension research: Implications for instruction. *Educational Psychology Review, 14*, 47–69; McDermott, L.C., Rosenquist, M.L., & van Zee, E.H. (1987). Student difficulties in connecting graphs and physics: Examples from kinematics. *American Journal of Physics, 55*, 503–513.

"appeared" in the mental image they created). Deeply processing both sorts of information vastly improved their memories.

A huge amount of research has shown that people remember concrete words (which name objects, such as "car," "tree" and "book") better than abstract words (which name concepts or ideas, such as "truth," "beauty" and "integrity"). Evidence indicates that people spontaneously may visualize the objects named by concrete words, but not the entities named by abstract words—and it's the addition of the visual information that allows us to recall the concrete words better.[66]

The Principle of Dual Coding can be extended even beyond mental imagery: This principle is really about showing plus telling. You can show things in many different ways, such as by demonstrations (as often occur in the sciences), by inducing people to move in specific ways (and thereby obtain kinesthetic feedback, which is a different kind of perception), or just by having them witness an event. Anything that engages both language and perception (visual, auditory, etc.) is going to boost learning.

This principle can easily be engaged using visual and auditory images during online learning, either synchronous or asynchronous. The key is simply to show and tell. You can illustrate what is being described at all three phases of the Learning Sandwich, during the lecture component, the active learning component, and during debriefing. And this principle can be especially powerful when it is used to induce deep processing, as occurs when students must actively locate or create illustrations or must create mental images.

In short, active learning exercises should take advantage of the Principle of Dual Coding, leading students to create or otherwise pay attention to and use both verbal and perceptual information.

---

66 Paivio, A. (1971). *Imagery and verbal processes*. New York: Holt, Rinehart, and Winston.

—7—

Deliberate Practice

fter accepting a job to teach in France, I was keen to learn to speak the language. I soon realized that I was not good at noticing the nuances of what I heard and was having trouble learning to pronounce French words. Thus, I found a native speaker who was willing to work as a tutor. It turned out that I was able to overcome (largely) this issue by using a simple technique: I tried to say a word or phrase in French, and my tutor then repeated it back with the proper accent. I listened very carefully, and said it again, trying to reduce the difference between what I had said initially and what she had then said. We often repeated this process several times with the same word. Although often slightly frustrating, my pronunciation did get better and I was (largely) understandable once I finally arrived at my new job.

This way of learning makes use of the Principle of Deliberate Practice, which states that "Learning is enhanced by paying attention to feedback and using it to update your knowledge and subsequent behavior." This principle requires students first to demonstrate knowledge by behaving in a particular way, then to receive specific feedback about the correct behavior, then to pay attention to the difference between their first effort and the correct version, and finally to update their knowledge in order to improve subsequent behavior.[67] All the while, students are processing deeply the material they need to learn.

---

67 Brown, P. C., Roediger, H. L. III, and McDaniel, M. A. (2014). *Make it stick: The science of successful learning.* New York: Belknap Press; Ericsson, K. A., Krampe, R. T., & Tesch-Romer, C. (1993). The role of deliberate practice in the acquisition of expert performance. *Psychological Review, 100,* 363-406.

Critically, the feedback must address a specific behavior, must be concrete, and must be provided as soon as possible after the behavior. The feedback must identify exactly what needs to be improved and should indicate how to improve it.[68] Just saying "pretty good" is not effective because this doesn't tell the student which aspects of what they did were good and which were not. (This reminds me of a story I heard about the filming of one of the early Star Wars movies: After a take, the director told the cast "Do it again, only better." They did not find this very useful.) Crucially, the feedback should not address their failings as a human being, but instead focus on what they need to do to improve.

Let's deconstruct this process:

1. The first thing a student needs to do is to demonstrate knowledge in some way, by doing something. In my French example, my behavior usually was my trying to say a French word. But this principle applies to almost any aspect of knowledge or skills that students can demonstrate; for example, the behavior could be a golf swing, writing some computer code, or giving a speech.

2. The next step is to receive feedback, which typically is an example of the correct (or vastly better) version of what the student tried to do—a native speaker saying the word, an expert coach demonstrating the golf swing, and so forth. However, in some cases the feedback may not be the correct version of the entire behavior, but instead may zero in on specifically what was incorrect, helping the student to identify what needs improvement. For example, instead of repeating back the word, my French teacher might have focused just on the "r" sound that I was doing incorrectly.

3. Crucially, students need to pay close attention to the correct behavior and notice the disparity between what they did and what they should have done.

4. And finally, students need to use that observation to update how they think about what they should do—which will affect their performance in the future.

Deliberate practice stands in stark contrast to mindless practice, which is just doing something over and over again and hoping to improve—which is not very effective. With deliberate practice, students need to pay close attention at every step of the way and make a deliberate effort to reconceive what they are doing. This is difficult: Students need to keep in mind their first try, the feedback, what's

---

68 Hattie, J., & Timperley, H. (2007). The power of feedback. *Review of Educational Research, 77,* 81-112; Kluger, A. N., & DeNisi, A. (1998). Feedback interventions: Toward the understanding of a double-edged sword. *Current Directions in Psychological Science, 7,* 67–72.

different between their first try and the feedback, and then need to adjust their next attempt.[69]

Figure 7.1 Steps of Deliberate Practice

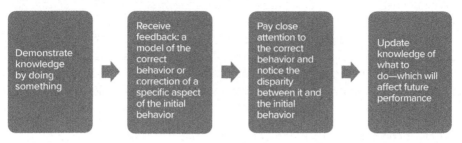

For deliberate practice to be most effective, students need to venture outside their comfort zone—they need to push themselves to do something they find difficult and persist in trying (and trying again) to improve. in deliberate practice, students focus mainly (or only) on the parts that they need to improve; this can be frustrating because they are continually falling short as they learn. In my French example, I didn't repeat words that I already pronounced clearly, I only focused on the words I had difficulty with—which can be demoralizing. In fact, deliberate practice requires that students make errors, which are then corrected.[70] However, deliberate practice won't work if students reach too far outside their comfort zone. Again, the new material must not be so easy as to be boring or so difficult as to be frustrating; you need to aim for the "Goldilocks spot."[71]

The problem is that this Goldilocks spot is different for different people. If deliberate practice is administered in breakout groups, as I discuss shortly, I again recommend using groups composed of students who have comparable relevant abilities. If heterogeneous groups are used, some students will find the task more challenging than others and may hesitate to put themselves in a situation where they might fail when they are with others who don't seem to be having a problem.

---

69 Ericsson, K. A., Prietula, M. J., & Cokely, E. T. (2007, July-August). The making of an expert. *Harvard Business Review*: https://hbr.org/2007/07/the-making-of-an-expert

70 Mayer, R. E. (2008). *Learning and instruction*. Upper Saddle River, New Jersey: Pearson Education, Inc.

71 For a more general statement of the utility of pushing students a bit beyond their comfort zones, see Bjork, E. L., & Bjork, R. A. (2011). Making things hard on yourself, but in a good way: Creating desirable difficulties to enhance learning. In M. A. Gernsbacher, R. W. Pew, L. M. Hough, J. R. Pomerantz, & FABBS Foundation (Eds.), *Psychology and the real world: Essays illustrating fundamental contributions to society* (p. 56–64). New York: Worth Publishers.

Selectively Paying Attention

To use deliberate practice effectively, the students must pay attention to the relevant aspects of what they are trying to learn. Helping them to do this is one role of the instructor. Over time, students may learn what to pay attention to, and then be able to direct their attention independently, without needing an instructor. For example, ear training requires paying attention to the pitch (the musical note, such as C or E) and not the timbre (the "color" or "texture" of a note—as illustrated by the difference between the same note being played on a piano versus on an organ). Another example: When I was learning French pronunciation, I needed to pay attention to the particular sound of the "r" and to the purity of vowels.

One technique that can lead students to pay attention to the appropriate aspect of what they are learning is "interleaving." Researchers have found that mixing up different types of cases from the same general category is generally a better way to learn than "blocking" together all the different types of cases.[72] For instance, if the goal is to teach students to identify paintings by specific artists, it's better to ask them to study paintings by different artists (e.g., Braque, Seurat, and Wexler) interleaved than to study each artist's work one at a time. (Of note, when asked afterwards, participants believed that mixing up the artists was less effective than studying them one at a time—which is the opposite of what the researchers actually found, and again should make us cautious about accepting our intuitions about how people learn best.) Mixing up the examples leads students to compare and contrast them, which helps them to learn the distinctive characteristics of each artist's style.[73] By interleaving, you lead students to recognize what they need to focus on when they then engage in deliberate practice.

However, a word of caution: Interleaving is better than blocking only after students have enough knowledge about each of the to-be-learned categories to be able to make the necessary distinctions. For example, studies have shown that when first learning pronunciation of foreign words, students do better when they learn words with the same pronunciation together, rather than being intermixed with words that have different pronunciations.[74] When just getting off the ground, the main problem is to get the basic idea of how the novel vowels

---

72 Pan, S. C. (2015, Aug 4). The interleaving effect: Mixing it up boosts learning. *Scientific American:* https://www.scientificamerican.com/article/the-interleaving-effect-mixing-it-up-boosts-learning/; Rohrer, D. (2012). Interleaving helps students distinguish among similar concepts. *Educational Psychology Review, 24,* 355–367.

73 Kornell, N., & Bjork, R. A. (2008). Learning concepts and categories: Is spacing the "enemy of induction"? *Psychological Science, 19,* 585-592.

74 Carpenter, S. K., & Mueller, F. E. (2013). The effects of interleaving versus blocking on foreign language pronunciation learning. *Memory & Cognition, 41,* 671-682.

and consonants sound, which is a prerequisite for making distinctions among them. If students have no idea what to pay attention to in order to distinguish among categories, mixing up different types of examples may just be confusing.

Interleaving is a special case of a more general technique, which simply requires students to make comparisons and contrasts. The key is to have a model (the correct behavior, fact, concept, image, procedure, etc.) of what should be learned and to contrast it with other examples that differ from the model in only a single way. By noticing the differences between the model and near-misses, students learn what to pay attention to when refining their knowledge and behavior.[75] For instance, if you wanted students to learn to pronounce Spanish properly, you might have them listen to a series of words that were pronounced correctly or incorrectly, and they would need to identify which was which. The trick is to have the incorrect words differ in a minimal way from the correct ones. This procedure will sensitize students to the sounds that they should produce. Going back to teaching the styles of different artists, you could pair a genuine example with a version that differs in subtle ways, and students have to pick out which is which—and receive feedback, which directs them to pay attention to distinctive characteristics. In fact, an art museum actually did this, pairing originals with forgeries![76]

Another technique that can help students learn what to pay attention to when they then engage in deliberate practice is called shaping.[77] Shaping occurs when you start with a very broad distinction, provide feedback until students master it, and then narrow it down, repeating the process until you reach the appropriate level of precision. For example, when conducting ear training, an instructor may initially simply want students to distinguish notes that are higher versus lower in pitch. The instructor might start with notes that are separated by an octave, which is very easy, and then go to a fifth, and then to a third, and then to a second and finally a semitone.

Deliberate Practice at Scale

Deliberate practice is difficult to implement at scale. The traditional way to help students engage in deliberate practice is to have a tutor or coach work with each individual student. This is what my French tutor did, what golf coaches do, what

75 Bransford, J. D., & McCarrel, N. S. (1974). A sketch of a cognitive approach to comprehension. In W. Weimer & D. S. Palermo (Ed.), *Cognition and the symbolic processes*. (pp. 189-229). Hillsdale, NJ: Erlbaum Associates.

76 Gardner, H. (1982). *Art, mind, and brain: A cognitive approach to creativity*. New York: Basic Books.

77 See Kosslyn, S. M., & Rosenberg, R. S. (2020). *Introducing psychology: Brain, person, group (5th edition)*. Boston, MA: FlatWorld.

expert surgeons training medical residents do, and so on. However, this sort of individualized tutoring is expensive and gifted tutors are often hard to find. Part of the problem is that experts often are not good at teaching their field: Their expertise has led them to forget what is obvious versus difficult for novices. To give high-quality feedback, the tutor needs to understand the sorts of errors that an expert no longer makes. And the problem is worse than that: The process of becoming an expert involves converting a lot of declarative knowledge to automatic, unconscious procedural knowledge—and thus experts may not even be aware of how they actually perform tasks in their field of expertise. (As a familiar example, if you are an expert driver, you probably are not aware of how you know how to steer your car—you just "do it.") In fact, studies have shown that "when experts in many different subject-matter areas teach or train, they leave out approximately 70 percent of the knowledge required to perform adequately."[78] Such incomplete instruction clearly impairs student learning.[79]

The good news is that tutors can be effective by relying on "cognitive task analysis" instead of expertise.[80] Cognitive task analysis consists of analyzing what people need to do at every step of the way when they carry out a task; it involves chunking by identifying the specific component actions that underlie a task. And then each of these components (and the relations among them) can be treated as specific learning objectives.

The first step to using deliberate practice at scale is to define the learning objectives very specifically. The second step is to have a standard or model that can be used to correct errors. This standard or model need not be presented by a human. For example, Benjamin Franklin learned to write well by studying an article he found particularly compelling, and then a few days later he would write it down in his own words. He then compared his version with the original, and noted the differences between the original and his version. He used this process to identify specific things he needed to do in order to improve his own writing.[81]

---

78 Clark, R. E. (2011). The impact of non-conscious knowledge on educational technology research and design. *Educational Technology, July-August*, 3-11, p. 4.

79 Clark, R. E.,Yates, K., Early, S., & Moulton, K. (2010). An analysis of the failure of electronic media and discovery-based learning: Evidence for the performance benefits of guided training methods. In K. H. Silber & W. R. Foshay (Eds.), *Handbook of improving performance in the workplace. Volume I: Instructional design and training delivery* (pp. 263–297). San Francisco: Pfeiffer.

80 Velmahos, G. C., Toutouzas, K. G., Sillin, L. F., Chan, L., Clark, R. E., Theodorou, D., & Maupin, F. (2004). Cognitive task analysis for teaching technical skills in an inanimate surgical skills laboratory. *The American Journal of Surgery, 18*, 114–119.

81 See Franklin, B. (1909/2016). *The autobiography of Benjamin Franklin.* C. W. Eliot (Ed.). New York, NY: P. F. Collier & Son. https://www.gutenberg.org/files/148/148-h/148-h.htm

Similarly, when learning to draw, you can take a photo of an object, try to draw it from memory, and then compare your drawing to the photo. Noting where your drawing deviates from the photo, you can then try again, repeating the process until you have fixed all of the glitches.[82]

In many cases students actually can provide their own feedback. At first blush, this may seem paradoxical; if they know enough to identify what they are doing wrong, why can't they use that knowledge to do it right in the first place? This strikes to the heart of a fundamental fact about learning: We often can recognize something even when we cannot recall it. As noted in Chapter 2, recognition occurs when you see, hear or otherwise perceive something that matches something you've previously stored in your long-term memory banks, so you can identify it and have access to associated information. In contrast, recall is when you dig something out of your memory banks and bring it to short-term memory (i.e., become aware of it) or produce something based on it. A critical difference is that recall requires digging the information out of long-term storage, which is much harder than simply matching what you perceive to memories of what you have previously encountered.

In many cases people may have a model stored in long-term memory and can use it to recognize how they should be doing something. By comparing current behavior to this stored model, people can note what they are doing wrong even if they can't immediately produce the correct behavior. (This can be extremely frustrating! You know you know it, but for some reason cannot use that knowledge simply to do it correctly.) Many highly accomplished people have described how they have given themselves feedback based on recognition, and then used that feedback to improve their recall and production. For example, Winston Churchill was known for his powerful and eloquent speeches, which he honed by giving them to himself first, in front of a mirror. Similarly, professional golfers may practice a course before a tournament; as part of that practice, they take many shots on the same hole, comparing and contrasting what worked and what didn't. This process allows them to update their knowledge so that they later can perform better in the tournament, when the chips are down.

In order to use Churchill's technique, you need both to recognize when you've gone off track and know the necessary corrective action. But even if you don't know how to fix the problem (as professional golfers probably do when they get a shot wrong), this process can be valuable: It directs you to learn what you need to know to fix that particular problem.

---

82 Scott Young, in his excellent book *Ultralearning* (2019, Collins Business), describes how he used a similar technique to learn to draw faces. By repeating this process hundreds of times, he became remarkably proficient (see the illustrations on p. 20 of his book).

One straightforward way to provide the needed feedback online is to put students into pairs and ask them to give feedback to each other. This is particularly effective if they have access to a "gold standard" model (the answer, correct behavior, correct fact, concept, procedure, etc.). Let's take a page from Ben Franklin's technique: Begin by asking students to create a work product that demonstrates their knowledge of the material, and then have them use a model to refine it. To return to our familiar example, ask the students to list negotiation tactics and summarize how best to use each one. Then have pairs of students compare each other's work to a model (i.e., a summary of a negotiation that embodies good applications of each tactic) and note the disparities. Then have the students produce an updated list and descriptions from memory. The pairs work together to correct each others' initial efforts so that they correspond to the model. To motivate students, they could be told that they will be tested on exactly this material at some point in the course, not necessarily immediately after the exercise.

This approach overcomes the concern about having the blind leading the blind—the concern that the students may not know enough to provide the relevant feedback. The students don't provide the "correct" response, but instead only help to identify the disparities between what their partner did and what they should have done, based on the "gold standard" model.

If you want to take this one step further, you can group each pair with another pair, and ask the two pairs to check each other's feedback. This sort of arrangement can be done in some video conferencing platforms by using a spreadsheet to specify in advance which students are paired initially, and then you later can combine pairs of students into larger groups (e.g., in Zoom, simply by asking the members of some groups to join specific other groups); alternatively, in asynchronous settings you can set up email lists and send students the assignments, asking them to contact each other directly.

To ensure useful feedback, it is a good idea to select randomly some of the pairs to present to the class immediately after the breakout groups end (i.e., during the final "debrief" part of the Learning Sandwich). To encourage students to pay attention to this debrief, you can run a poll immediately afterwards, asking whether the students agree with the feedback—and then call on several students to justify their vote.

In addition, for some types of materials there may be another way to scale deliberate practice: Programming computers to score students in real time and provide feedback. This can work well in domains where there are clear right answers (e.g., algebra), but even here such programs have been criticized as providing only "shallow learning." One problem is that they don't allow students to explain why they make certain errors, and don't strike to the roots of any problems with their underlying understanding.[83] Nevertheless, at least in some domains these programs can be included as one component of scaling deliberate practice.

Finally, so far we have focused on synchronous instruction, with immediate feedback. On the face of things, deliberate practice might seem to demand real-time, synchronous instruction. We know that feedback is most effective when it is delivered soon after the person demonstrates knowledge. However, such deliberate practice can also be done in asynchronous settings.

For example, students can do much the same pair-and share kinds of activities with a shared Google Doc that they can do in real time.

1. Students create a written or recorded work product that demonstrates their knowledge of the material; when it is complete, each student posts it in a secure location on the LMS (accessible only to the instructor).

2. In this case, however, it's not necessary to have students pair up in advance. Now, a bulletin board or shared document has been set up with pairs of slots, and students enter their name when they have posted their work product. If a pair of slots already has one name entered, the student supplies their name to complete the pair; otherwise, the student starts a new pair by entering their name as the first in a blank pair of slots.

3. When a pair is completed, you send the students the other member's work product and a model of an ideal work product.

4. The students then compare each other's work to the model, noting the disparities and suggesting ways to address them. All of this could be done either in writing or by leaving video clips for the other student to access.

5. Finally, the students are told that they later will be asked to produce an improved work product from memory, under proctored conditions.

As before, if you want to take this one step further, you can pair each pair with another pair, and the two pairs check each other's feedback.

As noted in Chapter 1, a variant of this approach is to have students enter days and times when they are available for a synchronous video chat. In this case, the students either select a partner based on the convenience of the timing or you could assign the students on that basis and send them email to set up the groups. This is a hybrid model, which relies on asynchronous creation of the work product and synchronous feedback sessions, which are set up asynchronously.

---

83 Intelligent tutoring systems. *Wikipedia*: https://en.wikipedia.org/wiki/Intelligent_tutoring_system

Figure 7.2 Asynchronous Deliberate Practice

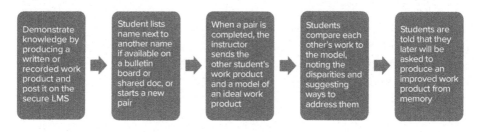

The methods described here can be used to good effect to help students hone their knowledge or skills over time. For example, writing typically requires multiple drafts and ideally the students receive feedback on each draft. Faculty, alas, rarely have the time to provide such feedback. By using the sorts of feedback techniques I've summarized here, students could benefit from performing several iterations on a work product and receiving feedback on each version.

Deliberate practice has been shown to be a very powerful learning principle, and it's clear that it can be exploited online. In fact, many of the techniques that are easy to do online, such as creating pairs of previous pairs of students, are time-consuming and awkward to do in a traditional setting. Moreover, deliberate practice can be provided at scale, in ways that give students feedback and an opportunity to improve relatively soon after they have produced a work product.

—8—

Combining Principles

The science of learning leads us to design activities that tap into how the brain learns. The principles summarized in the previous chapters generally reflect the operation of distinct brain systems. In fact, the Principle of Dual Coding rests on the idea that drawing on separate brain systems—one involved in language and the other involved in perception—gives the person two ways to learn something. We can move this idea up a level and identify ways to use all of the different principles in combination.

The "ICAP hypothesis" is an especially well-worked-out and empirically buttressed method that draws on combinations of the learning principles.[84] The key idea here is that students will be increasingly engaged by shifting between four modes. Specifically, the hypothesis is that students learn most effectively in *Interactive* activities (e.g., having novel dialogues that include answering questions and elaborating on what the other person said). Such activities will draw on deep processing, associations, chunking (e.g., if multi-part questions are used or complex topics are addressed), deliberate practice (if students receive corrective feedback) and even dual coding (if they use audio/visual aids). Not quite as good as this Interactive mode, *Constructivist* activities (e.g., explaining

---

84 Chi, M.T.H., Adams, J., Bogusch, E.B., Bruchok, C., Kang, S., Lancaster, M., Levy, R., McEldoon, K., Stump, G.S., Wylie, R., Xu, D., & Yaghmourian, D.L. (2018). Translating the ICAP theory of cognitive engagement into practice. *Cognitive Science, 42* 1777-1832. doi:10.1111/cogs.12626; Chi, M. T. H., & Wylie, R. (2014). The ICAP framework: Linking cognitive engagement to active learning outcomes. *Educational Psychologist, 49*, 219-243.

a solution to a problem in their own words, adding inferences as appropriate, or drawing a Mind Map) still draw on combinations of the principles effectively. Less effective than Constructivist activities, simple *Active* processing (e.g., mixing chemicals in a standard course lab in chemistry) can still produce learning, particularly when deep processing and associations are induced. Finally, all three of these modes are better than *Passive* processing (e.g., listening to a lecture without taking notes).

The idea is that students learn increasingly well as they shift to a more challenging mode, which makes sense from the present perspective: Not only do students mentally process information more deeply as they move into the more challenging modes, but they also are led to draw on and establish new associations, experience feedback that leads to deliberate practice, and so forth.

One interesting aspect of the ICAP hypothesis is that it suggests that different types of active learning exercises may be appropriate for students at different phases along their learning journey. Students who are just starting to learn a topic cannot leap into the most challenging mode all at once. This is one reason why we should consider a wide range of different kinds of exercises that can be used in active learning.

One specific type of active-learning exercise that induces combinations of the principles is mnemonic techniques, which are methods that boost memory.[85] These techniques can be used to help students learn knowledge or skills. The classic example of a mnemonic is the "Method of Loci." This method supposedly grew out of a gruesome event in Ancient Greece: A large banquet was in full swing when one of the guests was called outside to receive a message. Just after he left the room, the ceiling collapsed, burying all of the remaining diners under a heap of rubble. Spouses and tax collectors really wanted to know who had been in the room. The lucky survivor discovered that he could recall perfectly who had been present by using a simple technique: He visualized the room and shifted his "mental gaze" around the table, recognizing the diners one by one.

This basic method was refined over time and evolved into a set of related learning techniques. The Method of Loci has emerged as a way to use visual mental images to learn lists, collections of attributes or sequences of events— and research has shown that mnemonics that involve visual images typically are more effective than purely verbal ones.[86] To try this out for yourself here's what

---

85 Foer, J. (2011). *Moonwalking with Einstein: The art and science of remembering everything.* New York: Penguin Press.

86 Bower, G. H. & Winzenz, D. (1970), Comparison of associative learning strategies. *Psychonomic Science, 20,* 119–120.

you can do: Go along a familiar route, say from your home to where you work. Identify ten or so distinctive locations along the way, such as a mailbox on the corner, an impressive oak tree, a church, and so on. Once you've memorized the places (the "Loci"), you are ready to use the method. When you want to learn a sequence of items, such as a shopping list, all you need to do is to mentally revisit the route and leave a mental image of a to-be-learned item in each successive location. For instance, to learn the list you might visualize a loaf of bread sitting on the mailbox, a roll of paper towels hanging from the tree, a six-pack of soda sitting on the church steps, and so on. Then, when you later arrive at the market and want to recall your list, you once again take a trip down memory lane: But now you simply observe the items you previously placed in your mental image, as you go from location to location.

This technique is incredibly powerful because of the way it draws on various learning principles. Let's go through the five principles and see how they are at work here:

- **Deep processing:** You need to engage in considerable mental processing in order to visualize the to-be-learned objects and figure out how to imagine each of them interacting with the objects at each location along the route.

- **Chunking:** You can break the route down into sets of three or four locations and group them. Moreover, you can set up multiple routes, going from one to the other, which allows you to remember an enormous amount.

- **Associations:** By associating the to-be-learned objects with locations along your familiar route, you not only organize the material effectively but also firmly lodge it into memory. And more than that, by taking your later trip down your visualized route you have a systematic way to recall what you learned—simply by "looking" in your mental image at each key location and "seeing" what you left there previously.

- **Dual coding:** By both naming the to-be-learned objects and integrating them into a mental image, you have two shots at later recalling the list—one visual and one verbal.

- **Deliberate practice:** To do this right, you should test yourself after you initially set up your sequences of images, using the written list as the gold standard against which to compare your memory. If you fail to recall some of the items, you should use the specific feedback to figure out a more memorable image or a better way to integrate the visualized object into the scene.

Mnemonics are an excellent way to learn much more than simple lists. For example, they can be used to help you memorize the points you want to make in a speech, in the correct order. They can help you learn the rules of the road in preparation for your driving test. They can help you learn the phases of publishing a book. And so on. However, they generally require time to use, both to store the information and to get it out of long-term memory. The good news is that if you use the information repeatedly, you eventually will no longer need the crutch of the technique—you will be able to access the information directly.

All mnemonics rely on combinations of the principles of the science of learning, but to different degrees. As you go through the following brief summary of other mnemonics, think about which principles are being drawn upon particularly strongly (yes, I am suggesting that you engage in active learning yourself!).

Visual mental imagery can also be used simply to help organize to-be-learned material. For example, if you want students to remember that three authors were contemporaries, you could ask the students to visualize a period scene that would cement the relationships (e.g., two of them dueling, using books instead of swords, and the third officiating). This scene could be funny, bizarre or off-color, if it helps to make the associations stick in memory.

Another mnemonic requires creating acronyms based on the first letters of to-be-learned words. A common example is the way that many people remember the colors of the spectrum: ROY G. BIV (which stands for red, orange, yellow, green, blue, indigo and violet). An active learning exercise could require students to generate memorable combinations of acronyms for specific to-be-learned material.

Other mnemonics involve taking the first letter of to-be-learned words and creating a sentence or phrase where each word begins with one of those letters. For instance, back in my youth I recalled the order of the planets by memorizing "My Very Educated Mother Just Served Us Nine Pizzas" (for Mercury, Venus, Earth, Mars, Jupiter, Saturn, Uranus, Pluto). With the demotion of Pluto to non-planetary status, the mnemonic now could be "My Very Educated Mother Just Served Us Nectarines."

Another mnemonic relies on rhyming, such as "30 days hath September, April, June, and November. All the rest have 31, Fine! February 28 except when 29."

I'm sure by now you get the idea. Asking students to use a mnemonic to learn something can engage them and be fun. However, this sort of activity is not always appropriate; it really depends on what the learning objective is. If the learning objective is to learn a set or sequence of material, from simple lists to complex procedures, these mnemonics are very useful. We need to define learning objectives in advance and then use the science of learning to design activities that lead students to achieve the sought learning outcomes.

Elaboration, Generation Effect, Testing Effect

Another technique that draws on combinations of learning principles is elaboration.[87] The key idea is to ask students to expand on what is given. For example, if you give students one of the functions of associations in learning (e.g., organizing input) you could ask them to expand on this by providing other functions (integrating information into long-term memory, providing retrieval cues) and ask them how the different functions are related.

You can also induce elaboration simply by asking students to explain "how," "when," "why," or "where," such as asking why an event occurred, how a concept can be used, or where a procedure might be used appropriately.

Elaboration clearly invokes deep processing and forming new associations, and can also invoke chunking and deliberate practice, depending on the specific nature of the task. Indeed, it can also involve dual coding, if the elaboration involves illustrations or mental images.

Elaboration works in part because it induces the Generation Effect, which is enhanced memory that results from retrieving and organizing information from long-term memory.[88] One way to induce this effect is to ask students to prepare to teach someone else. Think about the mental processing required to teach effectively: You need to process the information deeply, organize it, think about the associations you want to tap into (relying on prior knowledge) and the new associations you want to create, and think about how you will present the information (perhaps using dual coding). The Generation Effect also needs to draw on the Principle of Deliberate Practice: Preparing to teach, or actually teaching, isn't going to enhance learning if the material being taught is incorrect; thus, to be most effective, the Generation Effect needs to be combined with feedback about the accuracy of what is being taught.

Another technique that draws on multiple principles is the Testing Effect which is related to the Generation Effect. The Testing Effect occurs when people learn more by being tested.[89] Remarkably, people learn more by taking tests even when they don't get feedback on how well they did on the test; the mere

87 Pressley, M., McDaniel, M A., Turnure, J., Wood, E., & Ahmad, M. (1987). Generation and precision of elaboration: Effects on intentional and incidental learning. *Journal of Experimental Psychology: Learning, Memory, and Cognition, 13*, 291-300; Xiong, Y. Zhou, H., & Ogilby, S. M. (2014). Experimental investigation of the effects of cognitive elaboration on accounting learning outcomes. *Journal of Education and Learning, 3*, 1-16.

88 Bertsch, S., Pesta, B. J., Wiscott, R., & McDaniel, M. A. (2007). The generation effect: A meta-analytic review. *Memory & Cognition, 35*, 201-210.

89 Roediger, H. L., & Karpicke, J. D. (2006). Test-enhanced learning: Taking memory tests improves long-term retention. *Psychological Science, 17*, 249–255.

act of taking a test—such as trying to recall the material—improves learning. Such testing includes self-testing with flash cards or quizzes. The Testing Effect is most effective when the test is not too easy (e.g., so students get 90% or more correct) or too hard (e.g., so they perform only a little above what you would expect from guessing). Much of the testing effect may spring from deep processing; the mere act of trying to recall may strengthen the memory.[90] In some cases, however, part of the testing effect may be deliberate practice, given that students often do receive feedback after each response to a question.[91] In addition, there is evidence that part of the effect is due to giving students the chance to make new associations to the correct answer.[92] Moreover, recalling the relevant information repeatedly over time will reflect the benefits of spaced practice.

Games and Meta-Cognition

Another way to draw on multiple principles is to have students play learning games. In fact, many of the activities described earlier can be made into games that require deep processing. For instance, you can make a contest out of devising a mnemonic. Each breakout group does their best, and the final versions are listed in a doc. Everyone could vote for their favorite (but not their own—and not knowing the identities of the creators of the other work products, to avoid this becoming a popularity contest). You can ask students to explain their votes, which provides feedback to the students who designed the mnemonics. Such an activity would also engender associations that both organize the key characteristics of good mnemonics and provide additional cues to help subsequent recall.

As another example, if you have a problem-solving activity (e.g., solving problems in introductory calculus), you can make this into a Bingo game. In this case, students receive a matrix and a list of problems. Each problem is numbered (say 1-16, if you have a 4 x 4 matrix), and each cell of the matrix contains a different number (from 1-16, in this example). The numbers are randomized, and different students (or groups) receive a different version of the matrix. If this is a group activity, students can work together on each problem or each student can work on a different problem and students then check each other's solutions. The students check off a cell when they solve the corresponding problem. When the students solve any set that leads to a complete row, column or diagonal, they signal "Bingo" and win. However, before you declare a winner, the work

---

90 Karpicke, J. D., & Blunt, J. R. (2011). Retrieval practice produces more learning than elaborate studying with concept mapping. *Science, 331*, 772–775.

91 Butler, A. C., & Roediger, H. L. (2008). Feedback enhances the positive effects and reduces the negative effect of multiple-choice testing. *Memory & Cognition, 36*, 604-616

92 McDaniel, M.A., & Fisher, R.P. (1991). Tests and test feedback as learning sources. *Contemporary Educational Psychology, 16*,192–201.

should be checked by another group. If the original group made an error, they are disqualified. If they get it right, they earn bonus points toward their grade.

Another way that the learning principles can be combined is by inducing *metacognition*, which is cognition about cognition. Metacognition requires students to monitor themselves during an ongoing task, and to take corrective action when appropriate. They must observe what they are doing well and not doing well, analyze the causes of poor performance, and adjust what they do subsequently in order to achieve a specific goal. One way to track meta-cognition is to have students either "think aloud," describing aloud the steps they are engaging in as they perform a task, or write down such steps.

Clearly, metacognition involves an enormous amount of deliberate practice, especially if someone else (e.g., a group member) provides feedback on the think-aloud or written transcripts of the thinking process. However, a lot of the learning may come from the analysis phase, which involves first understanding exactly what must be learned—which typically requires chunking the task (breaking it into manageable segments) and deep processing. And additional analysis is required subsequently when students try to perform the task, where they need to coordinate the different segments together.

It is clear beyond a shadow of a doubt that active learning is highly effective. But students must be engaged in order for it to be effective; they need to process information deeply, make associations, and all the rest. Many students will do this out of interest, but some (who may be most in need of learning) may not. A perennial problem in education is how to induce all students to be engaged. We turn to this topic next, which affects everything that has come before.

—9—

Intrinsic and Extrinsic Motivation

The "flipped classroom" requires students to listen to lectures or watch videos at home and then do their "homework" in class, which allows them to interact and take advantage of the instructor's expertise when they need it most. The flipped classroom had its moment in the sun some years ago and is no longer trendy. The flipped classroom seemed to be a great idea, rooted in thoughtful analyses and astute observations. What happened?

One explanation for the loss of enthusiasm for this method is simple: Studies (and personal experience) have shown that many students don't keep up their end of the bargain—they don't do the required work prior to class.[93] This is particularly a problem with a flipped classroom because if students haven't done the work before class, they can't take full advantage of being in class.

The broad question is how to motivate students to do what they need to do to learn. For active learning to be effective, students must be engaged. Thus we need to consider how to get them, and keep them, engaged. If students don't

---

93 Horn, M. B., Salisbury, A. D., Ashburn, E., Schiener, J., & Pizer, L. (2019). *Parent learners*. Entangled Solutions: https://info.entangled.solutions/hubfs/Parent%20Learners%20-%20Insights%20for%20Innovation.pdf?hsCtaTracking=fe032a1c-af15-4130-85ad-e5529a939296%7Cfc508bd1-b0ca-4987-b009-16620e13f263

pay attention and participate, none of the science and artistry of course design will make a difference.

Fortunately, an enormous amount is known about how to motivate people to behave in specific ways, and we can easily apply this knowledge in the classroom. In this chapter, we consider two different approaches that offer useful insights and invite specific educational practices. First, we consider intrinsic factors, which spring from a person's human needs, desires and aspirations. Following this, we see how such intrinsic motivation can work in conjunction with external factors that affect motivation; in particular, we expand on the ideas of incentives and consequences, as developed in behavioral psychology.

Intrinsic Motivation

Perhaps the most influential modern theory of intrinsic motivation, and how it interacts with extrinsic motivation, is Self-Determination Theory (SDT).[94] "Intrinsic motivation" leads one to do something because it is inherently interesting and satisfying (for that person); in contrast, "extrinsic motivation" leads one to do something because of external inducements.

According to SDT, we all are born with a need to be competent, autonomous and to relate to other people—and these three needs form the backbone of intrinsic motivation:

1. The need to be competent leads us to want to experience mastery, and the sense of mastery can be enhanced by feedback from others. Studies have shown that when people receive unexpected positive feedback (verbal praise for their performance), this boosts their intrinsic motivation to do that task—and negative feedback actually undermines their intrinsic motivation.[95] From an instructional perspective, this need implies that students should be challenged and that helping them succeed will be motivating for them to continue, going forward. The need for competence also implies that students should receive feedback on their successes but should not be working specifically to obtain praise or the like (which is why unexpected praise is key).

2. The need to be autonomous leads us to want to have control over our lives; it does not imply a need to be independent of other people. The ability to

---

94 Ryan, R. M., & Deci, E. L. (2000). Self-determination theory and the facilitation of intrinsic motivation, social development, and well-being. *American Psychologist, 55,* 68–78.

95 Deci, E. L. (1971). Effects o f e xternally m ediated r ewards o n i ntrinsic m otivation. *J ournal o f Personality and Social Psychology, 18,* 105–115; Vallerand, R. J., & Reid, G. (1984). On the causal effects of perceived competence on intrinsic motivation: A test of cognitive evaluation theory. *Journal of Sport Psychology, 6,* 94–102.

make choices increases intrinsic motivation. Thus, whenever possible, students should be able to choose a course of action. This can operate at different levels of scale, from choosing a major, to choosing courses, to choosing a particular section of a course, to choosing what project to tackle in an assignment.

3. The need to relate to other people leads us to want to feel connected to others and to belong to a group or community. Social context plays a huge role in governing what people want to do and can both promote and impair motivation. This fact can be a particular challenge in courses on some video conferencing platforms that do not allow students to see each other, which deprives them of rich social cues and a feeling of belonging. It can be an even larger challenge in online asynchronous settings, where students may feel isolated. (I have made numerous suggestions in the previous chapters about how to deal with these challenges, such as by having students swap video clips for specific exercises.)

SDT focuses on conditions that promote or impair these intrinsic motivations. SDT is in fact a loose collection of six separate sub-theories, each of which focuses on a distinct aspect of motivation. For example, "Organismic Integration Theory" (OIT) was formulated to address the interactions between intrinsic and extrinsic motivations. This theory focuses on the circumstances that lead people to internalize what started off as an extrinsic motivation and to integrate that motivation into their sense of self. If a motivation comes to be internalized and integrated, it will subsequently seem to stem from internal factors, not external ones. The theory specifies different levels of internalization and integration into the self, with greater levels leading to an increasing amount of autonomous motivation. The need for relatedness figures large in this theory, given that social factors play a large role in this process.

One relevant finding for educators is that giving students a meaningful rationale for why they should do something that they do not find inherently interesting facilitates their internalizing the motivation—and, at the same time, this practice increases the students' engagement, motivation and learning.[96]

The implications for instructional design here are clear: Before an activity, be sure to tell the students the learning outcome you expect and how this fits into the overarching learning objective—and be sure that the students not only understand this, but also buy into your learning objectives. Better yet: Use active learning and ask them to explain why the learning objective is worth achieving! Students must see why it's worth their effort to participate, both because of the

---

96 Deci, E. L., Eghrari, H., Patrick, B. C., & Leone, D. R. (1994). Facilitating internalization: The self-determination theory perspective. *Journal of Personality, 62*, 119–142; Jang, H. (2008). Supporting students' motivation, engagement, and learning during an uninteresting activity. *Journal of Educational Psychology, 100*, 798–811.

value of what they learn now and the value of what they can subsequently learn on the basis of this foundation.

As part of this process, before an activity you should explain clearly to the students how they should interact to produce the work product you expect. You should give students permission to think widely and broadly, to disagree with each other respectfully, and to argue for their views—while still being focused on the learning objective.

Cognitive Evaluation Theory (CET) is another sub-theory of SDT, which considers how variations in competence and autonomy affect intrinsic motivation. One central idea is that intrinsic motivation is increased when feelings of competence are combined with feelings of autonomy. Students need to feel that they are responsible for competent behavior; they have to know that it was their choice and their actions that led to the positive result.

CET implies that after group work in class each student must feel that they contributed, either individually or as a key part of the collective. But more than that, CET implies that students will be more motivated if they are given a choice about the specific task they can perform. For example, if you wanted students to learn the concept of supply and demand in economics, you could offer a set of alternative tasks that would lead to the same learning outcome; such tasks could include creating a PowerPoint presentation to explain how to use the concept, outline a debate about whether supply and demand should be the sole factor used to set prices, write a critique of an argument someone else has written about this, create a Facebook post that explains the concept in a way that 8-year-olds can understand, and so on. A student could choose the task they prefer, and then be paired with another student who made the same choice; if there are enough students in the class, pairs of students could then use rubrics to provide feedback to each other for each of the tasks. Doing this online can make this procedure straightforward and not create a huge burden for the instructor.

A key aspect of SDT is that it recognizes complex and nuanced interactions among intrinsic and extrinsic motivations. It recognizes that different people find different activities intrinsically motivating, and thus you cannot rely entirely on intrinsic motivation while teaching a class. Moreover, SDT notes that much motivation must stem from the internalization and integration of what begins as extrinsic motivations.

In the next section we consider specific ways that extrinsic motivation can be built into instructional design. Even though the language is different, many of the underlying concepts are compatible: In particular, we must assume that students are ultimately motivated by curiosity, a desire to grow, and a need to become more competent, autonomous and related.

Extrinsic Motivation

One way to provide extrinsic motivation to students is to build incentives and consequences into tasks. That is, we can conceive of extrinsic motivations as the incentives to do a task well and the consequences of doing it well versus doing it badly. These two factors are joined at the hip: the incentives are simply the anticipation of the consequences.

For example, consider how incentives and consequences can be leveraged in the "Think-Pair-Share" active learning technique. In this technique the instructor poses a question to students, who then have five minutes to think about it on their own and then discuss it in pairs (each of which is in a separate breakout group). The pairs are asked to write a specific response on a shared doc, knowing that some will be called on to defend their responses when the class comes together after the breakouts end.

Although this Think-Pair-Share method is popular, it does have a major drawback: With large numbers of students, the probability is low that any given pair will be called on after the breakout groups end and the class as a whole reconvenes. Thus, many pairs will not receive feedback, which is important not only for learning but also to build feelings of competence. Moreover, the fact that there may not be consequences for doing a bad job reduces the incentive to perform well. One way to address this problem is to have students produce a work product by the end of every breakout group or series of breakout groups—something they have to do that will be graded. The consequences of doing a good versus bad job should be clear from the outset. In addition, it is important that each student's contribution be clear; this is important both to help the student learn and to further the process of internalization and integration of motivation that is emphasized in SDT. In this example, the work product is a summary of the consensus view that the pair reached, but written independently by each member. With larger groups, another way to assess each student's contribution is to have the work product include well-defined sections, each of which is prepared by a different student.

If you do such activities, it's crucial that the students know in advance why they are doing the activities: You must explain your specific learning objectives (recall from our discussion of SDT that providing a meaningful rationale for an activity both facilitates internalizing the motivation and also increases the students' engagement, motivation and learning). This knowledge itself can serve as an incentive to do well if students understand that learning the material will help them achieve their own goals. In addition, you should tell them in advance the specific sequence of events and criteria for evaluation (and hence give them the proper incentives); thus, if you are using rubrics for grading, students should be given them in advance: "Teaching to the test" can be a good thing if the test is well designed.

For a more complex example of how to apply incentives and consequences in active learning, let's go back to the example where we use a jigsaw method to conduct a debate to help students understand the pluses and minuses of a proposed new law that would fund all elections publicly (see Figure 3.1). In this exercise:

1. Some breakout groups (six students in each) prepare for the "pro" side and other breakout groups (six students in each) prepare for the "con" side.

2. After a fixed amount of time (e.g., 10 minutes), you break up each group and create new groups that each contain three students from one of the previous "pro" groups and three students from one of the previous "con" groups.

3. The six students in each of these new groups then debate the issue, and each side tries to convince the other and—at the same time—tries to identify the strongest and weakest arguments of their opponents.

4. Following the debate, the students individually have five minutes to write down those arguments, with a brief justification of their evaluation—and this will be graded and, crucially, the instructor provides feedback.

In this case, the incentive during the first groups—each of which focuses on developing either the pro or the con argument—is that the students know that they will soon be debating and don't want to look bad to their peers (drawing on the innate need for relatedness identified in SDT). And when they actually debate, the incentives and consequences lead the students not only to do their best but also to pay attention to the other side—knowing that they will need to identify the strongest and weakest arguments later. The consequences of doing a bad job will be a bad grade.

Different Types of Incentives and Consequences

The idea of incentives and consequences comes right out of behavioral psychology, which specifies four distinct types of situations that motivate people. However, the nature of the incentives and consequences can be closely related to SDT, with a goal of helping students to internalize and integrate the extrinsic motivation. The key is to keep in mind that you never want to coerce or force students to do anything; students need to understand why they are engaging in a specific task and how it is going to help them achieve their own goals—which may include eventually using the knowledge or skills to get a good job or have a more satisfying life. The specific incentives and consequences serve to remind students of their own goals and help to keep them on track.

In all cases, the instructional designer needs to understand the nature of the consequences of the student's behaving or not behaving in a specific way (the incentives are the anticipation of the specific types of possible consequences). These consequences are defined by two factors, whether the consequence is attractive or aversive and whether something is added or is removed from the present situation. We can think of this as a 2 x 2 table, as illustrated below. Consider each of the four combinations of these two factors.

Table 9.1 Types of Reinforcement and Punishment

	Added	Removed
Attractive	Positive Reinforcement (+) (e.g., More Money, Good Grades, Praise, Promotion)	Subtractive Punishment (-) (e.g., Salary Cut, Demotion, Privileges Removed, Status Loss)
Aversive	Additive Punishment (-) (e.g., A Fine, Demerits, Criticism, Public Shaming)	Negative Reinforcement (+) (e.g., Getting Out of Jail Early, Not Forced To Eat Bad Food, Allowed to Leave a Boring Meeting).

1. **Something Attractive Is Added:** When your actions produce something you want, this consequence is positive reinforcement for those actions. Positive reinforcement increases the likelihood that you'll do those actions again. For present purposes, it's worth noting that many of these positive consequences are social: Praise is an obvious example and so is getting recognition or attention from others. Positive reinforcement occurs in class when students contribute to the work in a breakout group and their fellow students clearly appreciate their contribution. Similarly, positive reinforcement occurs when a student provides the correct answer to a question in class and the instructor acknowledges this in front of their peers.

2. **Something Aversive Is Added:** When your actions produce something you don't want, this consequence is additive punishment for those actions. Additive punishment will decrease the likelihood that you'll do those actions again. Many of these negative consequences are social: Being "called out" for making

an error or saying something inappropriate are obvious examples, and so is being ignored or being the butt of jokes. Additive punishment also occurs in school when students are made to stay after class to do extra work. In general, studies have shown that although additive punishment can be effective in the short-term, it is not an effective way to change a person's behavior over the long-term.

3. **Something Attractive is Removed:** When your actions cause something positive to be removed, this consequence is subtractive punishment for those actions. Subtractive punishment will decrease the likelihood that you'll do those actions again. A classic example is when parents "ground" their children for a period of time. (Or, as the Beach Boys illustrated, "We'll have fun fun fun 'till daddy takes the T-Bird away.") Feelings of humiliation, regret and anger often follow a dose of subtractive punishment. In school, such subtractive punishment occurs if a student is demoted from being a leader of a group because of poor performance. Similarly, if a student was used to being in an advanced placement section, being moved down to a lower-level section because of poor performance is subtractive punishment. It's worth stressing two things here: The action must have caused the problematic outcome, and the person must perceive the consequence as negative. For instance, for some students, being demoted to an easier section might be perceived as a relief, not a humiliation—in which case, the consequence might actually be negative reinforcement, not subtractive punishment.

4. **Something Aversive is Removed:** When your actions cause something negative to be removed, this consequence is negative reinforcement of your actions. Negative reinforcement will increase the likelihood that you'll do those actions again. For instance, if you hate boring meetings and discover that volunteering to obtain and supply refreshments allows you to be out of the room much of the time, the act of escaping the meeting negatively reinforces your volunteering to do that—and hence you will be more likely to volunteer to do this in the future. The key term here is "reinforcement"—this is a good thing! The concept of negative reinforcement is often confused with additive punishment, but the two kinds of events are very different. When a person receives either kind of punishment—additive or subtractive— after doing something, they are less likely to act that way in the future. In contrast, when a person receives either kind of reinforcement—positive or negative—after doing something, they are more likely to act that way in the future. When something aversive is removed, people often feel a sense of relief, gratitude, or even, depending on the situation, vindication—which are reinforcing emotions.

Again, many of the consequences that are perceived as negative reinforcement are social. For instance, breakout groups can be set up to include students with comparable performance of the relevant knowledge or skills; if a student was regularly being put into a breakout group with other students who they didn't like, performing better could lead them to be moved to another group—which is negative reinforcement (something aversive was removed, which was rewarding).[97]

Different consequences clearly can affect future actions, both after they occur (as described above) and just by anticipating them. Incentives often work by leading people to try to maximize or minimize certain consequences. For example, we humans are more sensitive to the prospect of losing something we have than we are to failing to gain something additional—we have "loss aversion."[98] Thus, just anticipating potential loss—as occurs when a subtractive punishment is in the offing—can be highly motivating; we will act in ways to avoid that consequence. In general, actions are shaped by knowing what the likely consequences of an action will be: We will try to do things to maximize reinforcement and minimize punishment.

Going back to our jigsaw debate example (see Figure 3.1), where we had two sets of breakout groups (first preparing different sides of a debate, and then recombining students to conduct the debate), you can now see more precisely how the incentives and consequences worked.

- In the first phase, when students were preparing for the debate, they were aware of the potential consequences of not preparing—and both wanted to avoid the additive punishment of looking bad to their peers if they did a bad job and wanted to obtain the positive reinforcement of their approval if they did a good job.

- Following this, when students were put into new groups and engaged in the debate, they were motivated to identify the strongest and weakest arguments because they knew that they will soon be graded—and now wanted to maximize the potential for positive reinforcement and minimize the potential for additive punishment.

For a more complex example, we can return to an example from Chapter 3, which summarized a multistep activity to help students learn negotiation tactics

---

97 For a more detailed description of reinforcement and punishment, see Kosslyn, S. M., & Rosenberg, R. S. (2020). *Introductory psychology: Brain, person, group (5th edition)*. Boston, MA: FlatWorld.

98 Kahneman, D. & Tversky, A. (1979). Prospect theory: An analysis of decision under risk. *Econometrica, 47*, 263-291. See also Kahneman, D. (2011). *Thinking fast and slow*. New York: Farrar, Straus and Giroux.

(see Figure 3.2). Incentives and consequences are used at every stage to motivate students to process the information deeply—and hence be likely to learn it.

- At the outset, the students are in groups that represent a single type of stakeholder, and prepare to use two particular tactics to negotiate with the other stakeholders. Each student knows that they soon will be on their own, representing their constituency, and so they need to pay attention and learn the plan. If they don't, they would be embarrassed in front of their peers (which is additive punishment).

- In the second phase, when they do the simulated negotiation and try to infer and evaluate the negotiation tactics of the other three stakeholders, the students know that they soon will rejoin their initial group and will report on their inferences. Again, the social component is huge: Students are incentivized not to look lazy, stupid, or disrespectful to their team. Rather, they are motivated to appear competent (in SDT terms), which is a strong form of positive reinforcement.

- Finally, in the third breakout group, where students report back to their initial group about their inferences and evaluations, the students know that their inferences and evaluations may be presented to the class as a whole and want to look as good as possible, both to the instructor and peers. Again, being seen as competent is strong positive reinforcement. In addition, because not every group will be able to present, students know that you will ask them individually to write down their inferences and evaluations, and will grade those—which is highly motivating to students. Autonomous achievement is also a strong form of positive reinforcement.

Asking groups to report to the class at the end of the exercise (the final part of the Learning Sandwich) has an additional advantage: It provides an opportunity for "cooperative learning" assessments. One interesting technique is have students first take an exam individually, and then to meet with a group to discuss the correct answers, and then to have the students take the exam a second time individually.[99] In this case, the final grade can be an average of the first and second time the students took the exam individually. If students know that this is coming, they will want to listen so that they can participate in the group discussion—which will enhance learning.[100]

---

99 Schwartz, D. L., Tsang, J. M., & Blair, K. P. (2016). *The ABCs of how we learn: 26 scientifically proven approaches, how they work, and when to use them.* New York: W.W. Norton. p. 145.

100 For additional techniques and insightful discussion on cooperative learning, see Gillies, R. (2014). Cooperative learning: Developments in research. *International Journal of Educational Psychology, 3*, 125–140; Slavin, R. E. (1995). *Cooperative learning: Theory, research, and practice (2nd ed.).* Boston: Allyn and Bacon; Slavin, R. E. (2014). Making cooperative learning powerful. *Educational Leadership, 72*, 22-26.

Social Motivation Online

Both the debate and negotiation tactics examples combine intrinsic and extrinsic motivational factors. The key is to rely on social interactions among the students and with the instructor (capitalizing on the "relatedness" intrinsic factor identified in SDT). Using small groups is a good way to promote such social interactions. When you do so, be sure to:

- Give students permission to take chances and try out new ideas, encouraging them to be constructively critical. In general, try to establish norms that lead to an open culture for the course as a whole.

- Explain clearly the point of the activity—both in terms of the short-term learning objective and why that particular learning objective is worth achieving.

- Ask students to produce a concrete work product by the end of the activity. This does not need to be a formal written report; for example, it can be a bulleted list of arguments used in a debate, or a set of images found on the internet, or solutions to a problem, and so on.

- Describe in detail the incentives and consequences by explaining in advance the entire sequence of events. Many of the incentives will depend on students knowing what is coming next, and hence being motivated to prepare for it.

- Provide feedback on the work product. If you do not, students will be less motivated to take assignments or activities seriously in the future. Keep in mind that the feedback should identify what they are doing well as well as areas for improvement; try to increase feelings of competence and autonomy (which are at the core of SDT). You can also use one of the group-based grading techniques to promote cooperation.

Relying on a combination of intrinsic and extrinsic motivations affects how engaged students are in an activity, which in turn has a large influence on how much the students actually learn.

The next chapter contains a catalog of many different types of active learning exercises. In almost every case, combinations of learning principles will be drawn upon. You should keep in mind how best to rely on intrinsic and extrinsic motivation. The aim is to design specific exercises with the learning principles in mind and to try to maximize their efficacy. If you use such exercises and motivate the students to be engaged in them, you will stack the deck in favor of the students' learning.

—10—

Exercises and Activities

When things don't change, or change only slightly, we humans begin to tune them out—and why not, there's little or no new information there. In order to keep students engaged, it's good to have many and varied types of active learning exercises. Fortunately, a wide range of active learning methods have been developed over the years,[101] and many of them can be effective online. In fact, many of the activities I summarize below can actually be more effective online than in traditional settings.

The first section of what follows provides many examples of specific exercises. Following this, I describe active learning formats that can be used online, most of which can be used for each of the specific exercises summarized in the first section. I sketch out how each format can work online in both synchronous and asynchronous settings. Every one of these exercises and activities is designed to draw on the principles from the science of learning.

Specific Exercises

The specific way that a particular exercise is used depends on the learning objectives, which depends (among other things) on the subject matter being

---

101 For example, see: https://cft.vanderbilt.edu/wp-content/uploads/sites/59/Active-Learning.pdf; https://cetl.uconn.edu/active-learning-strategies/#; https://poorvucenter.yale.edu/ActiveLearning; https://en.wikipedia.org/wiki/Active_learning

taught. The following list is intended to prime the creative pump of the course designer; although this list is long, it is by no means exhaustive.

Analyzing and Evaluating

One group of exercises focuses on carrying out an analysis and, possibly, an accompanying evaluation.

Analyze and evaluate a video, story, artistic work, or other creation: Any product can be analyzed in many ways; the learning objectives should specify the dimensions along which the analysis should take place—which should direct the students' attention appropriately. In addition, you should specify the criteria for evaluating the work. For example, when evaluating a video, the goal might be to examine how transitions between scenes fit together, it might be to analyze changes in the lighting, it might be to analyze the way the story and visuals fit together, and so on. Both the relevant dimension (or dimensions) and evaluative criteria (e.g., in a rubric) should be included in the instructions to students.

Analyze and evaluate by annotating: An entire video, story, artistic work, or other creation may be too much for many students to get their arms around. One way to break this into manageable chunks is to ask students to annotate as they go along. This is easy to do if the document is in Google Docs, Word, PowerPoint, Slides, and other media that allow embedded comments.[102]

Analyze and evaluate a case study: This exercise is the backbone of many business programs. To be most useful, however, you must select case studies to make specific points and must make clear what criteria should be used to evaluate the material.

Analyze and evaluate a problem: The first step to solving a problem is to understand exactly what the problem is, and different ways to frame it that may be more or less useful because they invite different solutions.[103]

Analyze and evaluate an argument: Students are given an argument and asked to analyze it by identifying the underlying assumptions and determining whether the conclusions do in fact follow from the premises. In general, students should evaluate both the strengths and weaknesses of arguments, not simply accept them or dismiss them out of hand.

---

102 If the work is in a different format, students can use Hypothes.is or Perusall, or for video clips using VideoAnt (see Mintz, S. (2020, July6). Making online active. *InsideHigherEd:* https://www.insidehighered.com/blogs/higher-ed-gamma/ma

103 For many examples, see Kahneman, D. (2011). *Thinking fast and slow.* New York: Farrar, Straus and Giroux.

Analyze and evaluate a claim: A key part of critical thinking is analyzing and evaluating claims, whatever the source (e.g., pundits, friends, politicians or scientists reporting research results). Students not only need to learn to identify underlying assumptions, they also need to understand the strengths and weaknesses of the evidence that led to the claim.

Analyze and evaluate the muddiest point: When acquiring new knowledge or skills, some aspects will be more difficult to understand than others. It often is useful to identify these sticking points and evaluate the best ways to address them. For example, when learning a new algorithm, students may confuse iteration and recursion.

Perspective Taking

Asking students to consider material from multiple perspectives is one way to induce deep processing and will lead to useful associations. The following exercises can be effective ways to do this.

Debate: Debates are often simply "pro" or "con" regarding a proposition (e.g., "Country life is better than city life"). This exercise allows students to examine tradeoffs, and to consider the topic from multiple perspectives. Another form of debate gives students several alternatives (e.g., "Which is better, living in a city, in a small town, or in a rural area?"), and they must debate which one is preferable. This latter approach, although less common, can lead to a greater variety of different perspectives.

Role playing: Role playing games can be an effective way to teach; the negotiation tactics example from previous chapters (see Figure 3.2) illustrates one use of this technique, but many others are possible. Role playing can induce perspective taking particularly well if students are asked to switch roles at some point during the process.

Alternative stories: Taking a familiar story and telling it from the perspective of different characters can also lead students to acquire a more nuanced understanding of a fact or concept (e.g., telling the story of Benjamin Franklin's time in France from the perspective of one of his lady friends).

Answering Questions

The process of answering questions often draws on virtually all of the learning principles. Here is a sampling of techniques that require students to answer specific questions.

Scavenger hunt: Students are asked to find on the internet illustrations or works that fit certain specifications, such as something that shows a method for generating electricity or a hat that can be used to strain cooked pasta. This can be made into a game by asking students to find creative examples and then having teams use a rubric to evaluate each others' offerings (without knowing the identity of the members of the other teams).

Predict demonstrations and videos: Rather than simply showing students a demonstration or video of a phenomenon, stop it part way through and ask them to predict what will happen next—and to explain why. Then move to a "reveal," where you complete the demonstration or video, and explain; this exercise can be a powerful way to provide deliberate practice at scale. Note that this can be done asynchronously: Students would watch a segment of a video, and only are allowed to watch the next segment after they enter their prediction into a bulletin board or the like.

Explore simulations: In many fields, interactive computer simulations are available that allow students to answer questions about key material. For example, a simulation in astronomy might show the temperature on the surface of the earth allow students to vary the tilt of the planet and observe the consequences (most students erroneously think that the seasons result from variations in distance from the sun, not differences in tilt). Or a simulation might show planets orbiting the sun and students could perturb the orbit of one planet and see the effects on the others. Simulations are particularly useful if interactions or "emergent properties" (such as occurs in natural selection) are key to understanding a phenomenon.

Generate test questions: Having students write the questions they then answer provides two opportunities for assessing how well they really understand the material. This can be particularly powerful if you give clear guidelines about the characteristics of a good question.

Take quizzes, tests and polls: Much learning occurs when students take quizzes, tests and polls, especially when they receive feedback about the correct responses (and why they are correct). Such quizzes, tests and polls can be used as "concept checks," being inserted right after a chunk of a lecture to ensure that students understood the key ideas. In fact, if students know about an impending quiz or test, this can serve as an incentive for them to pay attention and prepare during the relevant activity that precedes it. The biggest challenge in administering quizzes and tests in both synchronous and asynchronous online settings is proctoring, but several online services exist to ensure that the student who takes the quiz or test is in fact who they say they are. Ideally, such quizzes and tests tap a student's ability to apply or transfer information, and are not a simple test of retention (which can be gamed by looking up the answers).

Explaining

The process of explaining something can be a good way to learn (this is the heart of the Generation Effect discussed in the previous chapter). Many types of exercises lead students to explain material; here are some examples:

Short written exercises: Asking students to write a "Minute Paper" (a very quick answer to a specific question) summarizing what they should have learned in the previous portion of class is a good way to assess whether they do in fact understand the material.

Explain facts, concepts or skills: Having students explain material to each other can often be useful. In this case, however, after students explain, they need to receive the correct answer and ensure that their explanation was in fact correct.

Explain why it's wrong: Give students multiple choice tests and ask them to explain why the incorrect alternatives are incorrect.

Illustrate facts, concepts or skills: Students can illustrate material either by drawing it, taking photographs, creating videos, or finding images online.

Create Mind Maps: Mind Mapping is an excellent way to have students organize the material in a way that others can understand (see Chapter 6).

Story telling: Creating a story can be a great way to learn material—but the story needs to be focused on the learning objective.

Create a podcast: The simplest way to do this is to dictate into the phone, however various tools are easily found online (e.g., Audacity and Anchor.fm).

Demonstrate a fact, concept or skill: Students can create their own demonstrations to explain material, which can range from writing computer simulations to a short skit.

Virtual poster sessions: Students can create and present slide shows (e.g., using the free Google Slides). This can be especially useful if they are limited to a few slides, which can be much more difficult—requiring more thought and deeper understanding—than if they can use as many as they like.

Problem Solving

A problem exists whenever you have a goal but an obstacle stands between where you are now and that goal. To solve a problem, you either need to remove the obstacle or find a way around it. If problem-solving exercises rely on one of the group-oriented formats (e.g., focused discussion) that are summarized in the following section, they can be good examples of "cooperative" and "collaborative" pedagogy.

Solve problems: Problems come in many shapes and sizes, and every field has them. Asking students to solve a problem can be a powerful way to lead them to learn.

Design and conduct projects: Any project worth its salt involves doing something new, and thus involves solving problems. Project-based learning varies along a dimension: On one extreme are completely unstructured "discovery" projects; on the other extreme are highly structured projects of the sort commonly found in a chemistry lab associated with a course. In my view, neither extreme is ideal. Unstructured discovery may or may not lead to useful learning and often is unlikely to lead students to achieve particular learning outcomes; highly structured projects are not motivating and often convey the wrong message (e.g., actual research is not like the cookbook exercises used in lab courses). A better kind of project is structured with learning outcomes in mind from the outset, but is open enough to encourage student creativity.

Design and conduct experiments: Asking students to design and conduct experiments can be an effective way to teach if an expert (typically the instructor or teaching assistant) provides guidance and feedback.

Design and conduct observational research: Students can learn to become rigorous observers, especially if they are taught about the sorts of biases that can pollute such research.

Design and conduct library or archival research: Students can learn to organize domains and to conduct systematic, goal-driven searches—and to use the results of such searches to refine further such research.

Analogies: To complete an analogy, students must figure out the relationship between two things and apply that hypothesis to two other things. For example, "Good Grammar : Writing Process :: Science of Learning : _____ ."[104]

Sorting: Asking students to sort facts, concepts, images, words, procedures etc. into categories can lead them to process deeply and figure out an appropriate chunking organization.

Parsing: A way to help students learn the organization of a domain is to provide an unformatted document and ask students to identify where paragraph breaks belong and where major and minor headings should go.

---

[104] For many different types of analogy exercises, see Heick, T. (2020, June 3). A guide for teaching with analogies. *TeachThought:* https://www.teachthought.com/critical-thinking/types-of-analogies/

Formats for Online Active Learning

Each of the following formats can be a vehicle for many specific exercises. Ideally, I would have presented a giant table, with each of the following types of activities being entries on the rows and each of the specific exercises being entries in the columns—but practical considerations prevent me from presenting such a table. Nevertheless, it is useful to keep this idea in mind; each of these formats can be fleshed out in many different ways.

Individual Work

Students can be asked to work on their own, such as by writing a short answer to a prompt, analyzing and evaluating a claim, or summarizing arguments in preparation for a debate. A challenge here is to ensure that they do in fact do the work alone, without help from friends or fellow students. One way to ensure this is to require them to know the information for a subsequent proctored activity, which they cannot do well if they have not completed the prior work (and this subsequent activity can be graded).

> *Synchronous setting:* Students do the activity on their own within a fixed amount of time. In such settings, it's good to warn students when they have two minutes left, and then one minute left, so they can wrap up their work.

> *Asynchronous setting:* Students do the work off-line, on their own at their own pace (typically within a limited period of time); when they are finished, they upload their work product to a shared folder on the LMS, a Google Drive or the like.

Focused Discussion

Simply having a free-form discussion does not necessarily lead to active learning. In contrast, a focused discussion is designed to address a specific learning objective, and the moderator nudges the discussion to stay on track so that students are led to think about relevant material and considerations. For example, a focused discussion could ask students to take a familiar story and discuss how it might be told from the perspective of another character, to discuss predictions of how demonstrations will come out, or to generate good test questions.

> *Synchronous setting:* A key variable here is the size of the group, which can range from the entire class to a group of just two students. In general, a whole-class discussion does not offer all students much opportunity to engage in active learning. It's not just that there's not enough time, but also that the time between opportunities becomes so large that students may

simply stop paying attention (and they know that the consequences of doing so may be minimal). A better way to have such a focused discussion is to put them in breakout groups, with a maximum of six students.

Asynchronous setting: Students can conduct a discussion by making entries on a bulletin board or shared document (which is exactly what often happens in daily life, over email, text, Snapchat, etc.). This format has several advantages: students can read and respond at their own pace and there's a written record (which allows them to review earlier parts of the thread). The main disadvantages are that there can be a long lag between responses and that nonverbal information is missing. This last problem can be addressed by using video clips instead of entries in a written record. Again, proper security precautions must be taken to ensure that these clips are view-only and can only be viewed by the relevant students and instructors.

Think-Pair-Share

Students are asked to reflect on a specific problem, issue, goal, topic, fact or claim. For example, they could be asked to explain why the American civil war occurred, create a story to explain why the Russian revolution occurred, or calculate how much money rum would need to cost to make the Triangle Trade profitable, given estimates for other key costs. After a few minutes, students are paired to share their thoughts and provide feedback. To be successful, the students must have a well-defined task, which could be performed more or less well according to well-defined criteria (of the sort that can be put into a rubric).

Synchronous setting: Students initially reflect individually for a fixed amount of time and then are put into two-person breakout groups. It is important that each student has time to share, and thus there should be a signal halfway through the allotted time, prompting the students to switch who is sharing. In addition, students should be given clear criteria to guide them in providing feedback.

Asynchronous setting: Students initially do the activity on their own, at their own pace (within limits—perhaps they are given a week to do this work). When they are ready to be paired, they look on a shared document, which has a list from 1 to half of the number of students (if there are 20, the list would be from 1-10); each entry has slots for two names. Each student looks for a single name (indicating that the person has not yet been included in a pair). If they find one, they enter their name next to that person and contact that person via email (or the instructor sends email to connect them). If they cannot find a single name, they then list their own name and wait for the next student who accesses the list. Once they are contacted, each member of the pair then summarizes their view, in writing or video, and they give each other feedback. Again, students should be given clear criteria to guide them in providing feedback. (There is a corner case: If there is an odd number of students, when only three are left, those three would be on a single line so that they form a group—not a pair—and engage in the same process.)

Extended-Think-Pair-Share

This technique allows you to take advantage of things that are relatively easy to do online but are difficult to do in a traditional classroom. After a pair of students in a Think-Pair-Share activity has produced a work product, pairs of these pairs can then be created immediately—and each pair evaluates how well the other one did. Such evaluations should be made with well-defined criteria (of the sort that can be put into a rubric).

Synchronous setting: You, the instructor, can create the original pairs of students at random, which is very easy to do on most videoconferencing platforms. Following this, it's easy to combine pairs of these pairs manually. Alternatively, if you want to specify pairs (e.g., based on wanting to ensure diverse pairs whenever possible), you can set up a spreadsheet in advance. If the video conferencing platform allows only one set of breakout groups to be set up per meeting, for the second phase you can simply ask some groups to join specific other groups (e.g., this is a feature of Zoom), you can either combine groups manually or you can create a new class session and use a spreadsheet to set up those groups in advance (and ask the students to click on the new URL at the conclusion of the first set of groups).

Asynchronous setting: You can set up pairs in advance and email each student the name and email address of the other member of their pair along with instructions (or this can be posted in the LMS on in a shared doc on Google Drive or the like). After the pairs have produced their work product and indicated that they are finished, you would then email them the names and email addresses of their additional group members (i.e., the members of the second pair that they will join), along with appropriate instructions. The students could interact via shared documents and/or by exchanging video clips.

Jigsaw and Extended Jigsaw

Jigsaw designs are logistically awkward in traditional classrooms, but can be easily executed online. Simple jigsaw designs have only two phases: Students initially meet in breakout groups, with each group dedicated to preparing one part of a multipart project or activity. These groups are then broken up and their members are assigned to new groups, where each new group includes one or more students (depending on the specific activity) from each type of the initial groups. For example, this process can work well for setting up debates (with initial groups preparing pro or con positions, and later groups then debating), role playing (with each initial group preparing a separate role, which then are brought together for an activity), problem solving (with initial groups focusing on different aspects of the overall problem), and so on. With large groups of students, you need to set up multiple instances of each type of group.

An extended-jigsaw is the same, except that the second set of groups can then be reconstituted back to the original groups, paired (as in an extended-Think-Pair-Share design), or broken up to create new groups. Depending on the specific exercise, the third phase itself can lead to yet another phase, and so on. The negotiating tactics example offered in Chapter 3 illustrated an extended-jigsaw design.

> *Synchronous setting:* For a simple jigsaw, with just two phases, you can set up a spreadsheet in advance to configure the original groups and can set up a second set of spreadsheet entries to specify how to break up these groups to create new groups. If the video conferencing platform allows only one set of groups to be set up in advance per session, you can simply show students a list that indicates which groups they should now join, you can rearrange students by hand (which is feasible if there are a couple of dozen students or so), or you can create a new class session for the second groups; in this case, a spreadsheet can be used to specify the second set of groups in advance. At the conclusion of the first groups, students would click on a URL to join the new classroom. The same process is simply repeated for extended jigsaw designs.

> *Asynchronous setting:* Again, you would set up groups in advance, but now students can simply be emailed the names and email addresses of their group members along with instructions (or this information can be posted in the LMS or on Google Drive or the like). A separate shared document (e.g., a Google Doc) is provided for each group. After the groups have produced their initial work product, you then email each student the names and email addresses of their new group members, along with appropriate instructions (or post this information, as appropriate). The students could interact via shared documents and/or by exchanging video clips. For extended jigsaw exercises, the same process is repeated for each additional phase.

Reveal Techniques

Reveal techniques depend on asking students first to struggle with a problem or issue. Often the challenge is at the upper range of what the students can do, but not so difficult as to be utterly outside their reach. By making the challenge difficult, students may come close to addressing it, but not close enough to be satisfied—which may motivate them to get closure by paying close attention to the next phase. After this initial struggle, students then receive a "reveal" where the answer or best reframing is discussed. Research has shown that students are more receptive to lecture-based material after having tried to solve a problem or resolve an issue on their own.[105] "Peer Instruction," discussed in Chapter 1, is a special case of this active-learning technique.[106] Peer instruction is very well structured to keep the focus on a specific learning objective and has the advantage that many "challenge problems" (in numerous fields) are available on the internet. To be concrete, the following examples describe ways to implement peer instruction.

> **Synchronous setting:** You present a puzzle and alternative answers at the outset, and ask students to vote for one of the answers; many platforms now provide functionality to set up such polls in advance (there are also many polling apps online, which could be launched in another tab). Following this, students can randomly be put into three- or four-person breakout groups to discuss the problem. You, as the instructor, and any teaching assistants should join groups randomly to listen in and drop hints. When the breakout groups end and the class reconvenes, the students take the same poll again. You would then share the pre- and post-discussion poll results and ask students who changed their minds why they did so. You then use those responses as a prompt for a brief lecture that provides the correct answer and explains why it is correct.

> **Asynchronous setting:** You prepare a recording in which you present the puzzle and alternatives and ask students to vote in a poll, which can be done asynchronously (e.g., by entering their vote into a shared document). After three or more students have reported in, you send them (or post online) the names and email addresses of the other students to form a three- or four-person group, and ask them to discuss their answers offline (using a written discussion thread or by posting video clips). You (as the instructor) and any teaching assistants can monitor the threads and drop hints. When students have had a specified number of email exchanges, they are sent an email that asks them to take the same poll again. You then allow them to watch a brief recorded lecture that provides the correct answer and explains why it is correct. Questions (and answers) can be posted to a shared doc or bulletin board.

---

105 Schwartz, D., & Bransford, J. D. (1998). A time for telling. *Cognition and Instruction, 16,* 475-522.

106 See Mazur, E. (1997). *Peer instruction: A user's manual.* Saddle River, NJ: Prentice Hall.

Every one of the exercises and activities summarized above was designed with the principles of learning in mind and can easily be implemented online to draw on those principles. This list of exercises and activities is open-ended; these exercises and activities not only can be tweaked and tuned in various ways, but also can be supplemented and augmented. There is no limit to the number and variety of such activities and exercises.

As I said at the outset, this book is intended to be a springboard—to help instructors help learners. I end this book with a hope that all readers found general guidance, inspiration and concrete assistance in how to make their online classes better. And I hope this book motivates you to ground your teaching in the science of learning, and to use it as a foundation for your own creative approaches to teaching and learning.

Made in the USA
Monee, IL
24 June 2021

72183586R00069